The Changing Dales

The Changing Dales

by

W. R. Mitchell

Foreword by
Alan Bennett

UPPER SWALEDALE

DALESMAN BOOKS
1988

The Dalesman Publishing Company Ltd.,
Clapham, Lancaster LA2 8EB
First published 1988
© W. R. Mitchell, 1988

ISBN: 0 85206 948 0

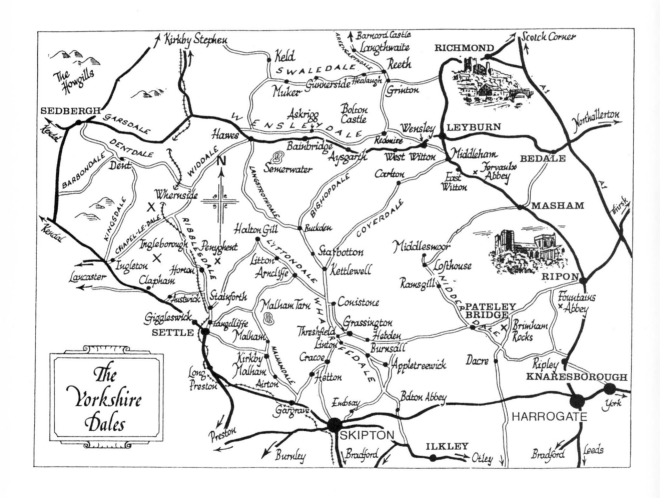

Printed by Fretwell & Cox Ltd.,
Goulbourne Street, Keighley, West Yorkshire BD21 1PZ

BOLTON ABBEY, WHARFEDALE

CONTENTS

VIEW THROUGH THE WINDOW OF THE RUINED CHURCH AT STALLING BUSK, NEAR
SEMERWATER.

PHOTOGRAPHS

All uncredited photographs by the author

HORSE-POWER AT HAYTIME

ON A DALES FARM

CATTLE AND SHEEP

A YEAR IN THE DALES

AN AGE OF LEISURE

HERRIOT COUNTRY

SHEEP-CLIPPER, SWALEDALE

FOREWORD
by Alan Bennett

IT'S IRONIC that Bill Mitchell's book should be entitled The Changing Dales. All the time I've known him, he's been the Editor of *The Dalesman* and this Yorkshire magazine doesn't change — or does so in such a way that you scarcely notice. Its form and contents, the cover, the recipes, the illustrations and the jokes — they're all as they were 30-odd years ago. And none the worse for that. "When it's not necessary to change," said the 17th century Lord Falkland, "it's necessary not to change."

Alas, that can't be said of the Dales themselves, and these days the pace of change seems to be accelerating. Barns are converted into homes (not always well); farms are turned into factories, the farmhouse being lost in a complex of featureless grey hangers; conifers creep up the valleys; quarries eat away the hills; and regularly, every week-end and holidaytime, all is swamped under a tide of visitors. Thank God for the sheep, I always think, because while we still have them we'll still have the stone walls they need for shelter.

No one is better qualified to talk about these changes than Bill Mitchell. Now retired from *The Dalesman*, he can draw on 40 years of experience in travelling the valleys and tramping across the hills, talking to all and sundry. He knows what a precious way of life we have here and how fragile it is. But he also knows that however beautiful and picturesque the scenery might be, the Dales are — and must go on being — a place of work. The two are not irreconcilable but the reconciliation can't just be left to chance, still less to economic forces. Regulation is part of it and a realisation of the fragility of the landscape is another.

This is a very special place. It has given Bill Mitchell his life and I think that in this book he is paying part of his debt.

Swaledale viewed from the road between Thwaite and Angram — a quintessence of Dales landscape with the simple, uncluttered form of a glaciar-hewn valley, ribbed by walls and with scores of field barns, each capable of being attended by one man, a horse and cart. The photograph, taken some 40 years ago, shows farmers with long-shafted scythes. Mowing a steep bank in a meadow may still have to be done by scythe, but elsewhere the processes of cutting grass and making hay are mechanised.

Thankfully, the herb-rich vegetation of many Swaledale meadows remains. A government grant encourages a farm with such to farm it in the old-time way, which means that modern fertilisers are not used. Some of the old-style hay meadows are seen by walkers on the Pennine Way near Thwaite. A rich and diverse flora marks them out from the fields that have been ploughed and re-seeded with ryegrass.

A MAN-MADE LANDSCAPE

NO TRUE WILDERNESS exists in the Yorkshire Dales. Wherever you look, the hand of man is apparent. Wherever you go, there is always the feeling that someone has been there before you. The weather is frequently wild. In blustery conditions the hill sheep find "bield" [shelter] in the lee of the walls, but conditions are transient; a shaft of sunshine appears, announcing another "bright period". The old Dales haymakers regarded as a good omen an area of blue sky "big enough to patch a Dutchman's trousers."

When the "mucky" clouds disperse; when the Dales appear with clarity and colour, man's effect on the landscape is apparent. Stand, as I did, where the Buttertubs Pass begins its descent into Swaledale, and notice the orderly appearance of the dale. Even the edge of the open fell is neat, the coppery hue of bracken ending abruptly at the straight walls of the topmost pastures.

Now look for the tatters of ancient woodland where the incessant grazing of sheep has prevented natural regeneration. The fields on the alluvial flats have a neat wall pattern and a proliferation of small barns — hundreds of outbarns in every lanquid view. The old grey farmsteads are part of this astonishing pattern of stone. Yet it is within 200 years old, a mere wink in the story of the Dales, that an ancient wall system was extended with the Enclosure Acts. Hundreds of miles of new walls appeared within a relatively short time; they stormed the fells, accentuating the contours. The drystone waller became a frontiersman, taking in areas of the moor and leaving it to the farmer and his stock to improve the ground.

It is estimated that in the Dales National Park there are some 10,000 stone barns, the majority of them being of the small field variety where a farmer kept perhaps a dozen cows the winter through, feeding them with hay taken from the adjacent land and turning out the cattle daily, sometimes in snow, so that they might drink at a nearby spring. I have counted over 300 barns in a single stupendous view of part of upper Swaledale, but the total number is some 800.

When officials of the Historic Buildings and Monuments Commission were in the Dales National Park in November, 1987, it was agreed that the (man-made) upper dale landscape is of international importance. Yet all is not well. Maybe a quarter of Dales barns are neglected to the stage at which they are on the point of collapse. When the less important walls become "gapped", a farmer who is short of labour and can obtain a grant for fencing is inclined to let the ancient boundaries go.

The hymn-writer lamented that "change and decay in all around I see." The legacy of unnumbered generations of Dalesfolk is under threat. Wind and weather are the ancient enemies. Gales lift roofing slates on the barns. At one time these slates were easily replaced from local quarries but none of the old type remains in operation. The barn that is not needed has its slates removed, to be sold to a house-builder. The role of dozens of outbarns has been taken over by a single huge building that is handy to the farmhouse; the cattle dine on silage. The new structure is often an eyesore but no planning permission was necessary.

Immense changes have taken place since *The Dalesman* was first published, in April 1939.

A FARMER AT KELD, HAVING HAND-CLIPPED A SHEEP, BEGINS TO ROLL UP THE
FLEECE.

In those days, traditional ways were evident, whether it be in farming or one of the craft industries. It was in the 1930s that a distinctive Dales way of life became eroded as the indigenous population began to decline and we became largely dependent on the goods and services of the town. The old 'uns among us, recalling those times, remember also the austerity. Most families had little in cash and kind. The villages were much shabbier than they are today, when high property prices ensure that even rabbit hutches are well-maintained.

The effect of change on the Dalesfolk themselves during the past 50 years has been striking. Those who survive in farming are fully mechanised, which means they employ little outside labour. Some have been persuaded to accept grant aid to maintain their old-type hay meadows and elsewhere the landscape is a tedious ryegrass-green, the grass being fed with "artificials" to yield a sappy growth for silage. In the upper dales, beef cattle of varied breeds have replaced the genial Shorthorn, which was dual-purpose, yielding milk for butter and cheese. The hill sheep are still a distinct Pennine breed; the lowland sheep have gone through changes in fashion.

In the villages, an ageing population is becoming outnumbered by "off-comers" — worthy folk, interested in the Dales way of life, but lacking sensitivity towards its finer points. Some 680 square miles of Dales country lie within the Dales National Park. In the Age of Leisure, visitors find thickets of signs, car parks, litter bins, information centres, wardens, greatly eroded footpaths, steps beside Malham Cove and a general hub-hub to which low-flying jets add their own distinctive waves of sound. Not only have most fields become flowerless, but conifer forests clag the landscape (in 1988 it was announced that no more would be permitted on the Pennine uplands). Small-time limestone quarries have become gigantic undertakings. Not only faith moves mountains!

The Dales have their "honeypots", like Aysgarth, Malham and Bolton Abbey. Elsewhere, visitors are well spread out and Dales life follows an unhurried course. Meeting an old friend at Keld, we spoke of the days when the folk of the upper dale were staunchly independent, demanding little of the outside world. They warmed themselves by a fire made of Tan Hill coal — "brittle, gassy stuff" — and with peat from the moors. The vet was called only to critical cases and it was all "bottle stuff", though the prescribed cure for swine erysipelas was holding the animal's snout in a bucket that contained hot water and eucalyptus. "I had to put a cloth round so that the steam went up the pig's nose."

The archetypal dalesman endures, with an individualistic approach to life and a deep love of his native "heaf" which he finds hard to express in words. The farmers of the upper Dales are still pre-occupied with the weather and with sheep. Recent news of the death of William Alderson (Bill Upsteps) of Swaledale, reminded me of the last time I met him. He remarked: "Its aw reet as long as thou doesn't get snawed up i' bed" and went on to tell me of the night when he left his bedroom window open, as usual, and an unexpected blizzard deposited several inches of snow in his room. A farmer living in Chapel-le-Dale summed up the local weather succinctly with words: "East wind for snow; west wind for rain."

I love the dalesman's ready wit and vivid expressions. Near Semerwater, a farmer referred to the two sides of Raydale — one side being on the "sunny side" and the other on the "money side". I heard of a man at the dalehead who, when asked about his large family, replied: "Aye, We hadn't so much to do up here of a winter's neet. It's different nah — they've getten t'telly!" J.B. Priestley, in his "English Journey", which was published in 1934, told of the woman living at a remote farm who each week visited the village of Kettlewell, in upper Wharfedale. She suddenly broke with custom, telling an inquirer: "I can't stand t'racket."

The Changing Dales is being published to mark the golden jubilee of *The Dalesman* magazine, with which I have been associated for 40 years. When I was about to retire as Editor, and Yorkshire Television made a half-hour film, Alan Bennett — who has a home in the Dales — agreed to be the narrator. He mentioned as a compliment the magazine's old-fashionedness, and also described it as "something like a parish magazine." The founder and first Editor, Harry J. Scott, would have been delighted.

Alan readily agreed to write a foreword to *The Changing Dales . . .*

Opposite Page: Hannah Hawkswell, of Baldersdale (Yorkshire Television).
Below: Buttertubs Pass.

ABOVE: WENSLEY, WHICH GIVES ITS NAME TO A DALE (Ron and Lucie Hinson).
BELOW: SEMERWATER, WITH AN ICE-BORNE BOULDER CALLED THE CARLOW STONE.

LIFE IN THE 1930s

HARRY J. SCOTT, who founded *The Dalesman,* became a dalesman himself in the summer of 1935 when, leaving a well-paid job on *The Yorkshire Post* in Leeds, he moved with his family to Clapham, in the shadow of Ingleborough. Claude Barton, agent of the Ingleborough Estate, rented him "a little house" at £21 per annum and agreed to install a new bath. Local electricians re-wired the house for £14 and the Settle Electricity Company made power available at one penny a unit. The Scott family engaged a removal firm to transport their possessions from Headingley to Clapham for seven guineas. The young journalist reckoned that if he could earn £3 a week, he would be able to live comfortably and also run a car.

The first issue of his magazine *The Yorkshire Dalesman* appeared in April, 1939. In his first editorial, Harry Scott had drawn an arbitrary line round what was generally accepted as "the Dales". He estimated the population at 350,000, adding: "Into the Dales there come each year, for pleasure and recreation, probably as many again, perhaps more. And all over the world are Yorkshire folk for whom this part of the country fills a big place in their picture of 'home'."

In setting up the magazine, he had the help of W.L. Andrews, Editor of the *Leeds Mercury,* an old-established newspaper that was soon to be merged with *The Yorkshire Post.* It was WLA who introduced him to worthy folk, including Marie Hartley and Ella Pontefract, who had been writing about the Dales since they had stayed in a rented furnished cottage at Angram, near Keld, in June 1932. In an article submitted to *The Dalesman* to mark its 40th birthday, in 1979, Marie recalled the peacefulness of those days. "It was possible to walk Dales roads and lanes all day and see no one but the occasional farmer going about his work . . . Only the buzz of a bee, rustling of grasses, the sad bleating of sheep and the bubbling call of the curlew disturbed the absolute silence."

In the 1930s, Ella Pontefract and Marie Hartley charmed us with their books *Swaledale* (1934), *Wensleydale* (1936) and *Wharfedale* (1938). I recall Marie Hartley telling me how in their early days they would listen to the recollections of an old dalesman and then, when out of sight, would hurriedly jot down all they could remember. In the 1930s, speech tended to be slow, reflective and containing little technical jargon. Ella, writing about "Dales Folk" in the very first issue of *The Yorkshire Dalesman,* noted the vividness of expression that owed much to dialect and was an attractive characteristic of the Dales at that time. She quoted what a Dalesman said of a small boy: "He were nobbut a peeat high." And she reported that a Daleswoman said to a camper: "Tha's nivver gaen to lig under yon' lump o' clout." Using a car-drawn caravan, which they parked in a field at Bainbridge, the two — writer and illustrator — watched men cutting and setting peat on the fells, for then many people burnt peat. An old lady of 80 told them that when she was a child her reward for setting the blocks of peat to dry was to be taken to Askrigg Hill Fair.

In the 1930s, as changes came to the social life of the Dales, Ella Pontefract found herself recording elderly folk. She commented: "It is not that individuality is lacking amongst the

EARLY ON A SUMMER'S MORNING AT MIDDLEHAM, WENSLEYDALE. THE RACEHORSE
WAS ONE OF MANY TO BE EXERCISED ON THE LOCAL MOOR.

young. Up and down the dale, young and energetic men are raising the level of dale farming, liming and draining neglected land, concentrating on pedigree stock, encouraging the Young Farmers' Club. But the old have a lifetime of memory behind them; they have known people whose names are worn now on the churchyard stones, and who lived in an era which has sunk into history. They belong to a time when the fells shut the dales in from the outside world and in a great measure from each other. They are reflections of their dale."

Indeed the 1930s saw the beginning of radical changes in the traditional life of the Dales, which had evolved in isolation and at one time was virtually self-supporting. In 50 years our way of looking at the Dales was to be transformed.

The Milk Marketing Board came into being in 1933. Farmers living within a reasonable distance of the railway had been accustomed to sending their milk in kits to the nearest towns, hoping that they would be paid for their produce. In the remoter areas, milk had been separated, the cream being used for making butter or cheese and the "blue" [skimmed] milk fed to the young calves. The Dales farmer now had the benefit of a monthly milk cheque; it rapidly became a cornerstone of his economy.

Young Farmers' Clubs were appearing in the western Dales in the late 1920s. The first to be established in Yorkshire was at Bashall Eaves (now in Lancashire). After a slow start, the movement became popular through its aim of providing the youthful population of the countryside with educational, social and to some extent, recreational facilities. I remember Mr. J. Robb listing among the aims the breaking down of shyness and reserve. This was largely to be accomplished through public speaking competitions. In due course, young men became so confident they were actually proposing marriage to girls from the next dale. In due course, those girls became members of the Women's Institute movement. Almost all rural women were connected with the WI, which had far more to its activities than "jam and Jerusalem".

In the 1930s, local bus services gave to the Dalesfolk an extraordinary degree of mobility. Hardly any of the local people possessed cars, which meant that distances were covered on foot or by bike. Before the 1939–45 war put restrictions on private motoring, there had been traffic jams in various places. Having been brought up at Skipton, I recall how crowded this "gateway to the Dales" became at week-ends, and especially on Sunday evenings. Sometimes, I visited a friend and saw his ailing mother sitting behind the lace curtains in the front room, watching the traffic moving in fits and starts. It was the most exciting experience of her week.

When the Rev. Trevor Woodd presided over the Oughtershaw estate, at the head of Wharfedale, the visitors for grouse-shooting arrived by train at Hawes and were conveyed over Fleet Moss in horses and wagonettes hired from Elijah Allen at Hawes. So infrequently seen were "posh" strangers such as these that children were instructed to bow their heads as the party passed.

In the Dales known to Ella Pontefract, all the farmhouses in the small branch valleys were occupied by different farming families. Oatcake in the old style was still being baked over the fire on a bakestone. Clogs were commonplace. "Haymaking proceeded as it has always done, slowly, with horses and wooden sledges and sweeps." Everywhere — sheep! Ella Pontefract used to say: "We shall never really understand the Pennine dalesfolk until we realise their pre-occupation with sheep." She quoted a Swaledale farmer who said: "Ah nivver count ma sheep. Ah ken ivvery yan i' t'flock."

The primitive way of life at a remote farm in the 1930s was described to me when I met Kit Calvert, of Hawes. He visited the Lamberts of Cam Houses, by the headwaters of Wharfe and Ribble. The journey involved travelling through Gayle and up to Fleet Moss, turning off the

A WHARFEDALE CELEBRITY: MAJOR HORNER OF "THE WHITE LION" AT CRAY, BEYOND BUCKDEN. MAJOR WAS A BAPTISMAL NAME NOT A MILITARY TITLE.

Wharfedale road to follow a track for a mile or two and then descending by a rougher route to where several small farms clustered together, as though for mutual warmth. One October, Kit and a friend who wished to buy a white cow arrived at the Lamberts' farm just after the pig had been killed, an event they celebrated by buying a gallon of gin. Most of the gin had already been supped. Kit and his friend were invited to drink some tea with "cream", the cream jug holding neat gin. In due course, they settled down to "bargain" over the white cow and offered Bob o' Cams £14 for it. He demanded £14.50 but eventually agreed to sell at the previous price — if the visitors would play dominoes with him for "a penny a pop". Bob soon covered the financial discrepancy and was well in hand. As the little group of dalesmen played, the October weather deteriorated. Mist settled on the fells — "we used to live in fog" — and there were flakes of snow in the mist. Soon the ground was powdered white. Kit and his friend left the farm with the white cow on a halter, which the cow promptly slipped, wandering off into the murk and snow. They had to return for the cow on the following morning, when conditions had improved.

A young man who delivered some sheep to Cam Houses was offered "a bit o' dinner" by Eric Lambert, one of the three bachelor brothers. There were some snags. Bob (the nomadic brother) had forgotten to buy "a bit o' beef" at Hawes, so they had eaten the "bit o' bacon". The hens had not laid any eggs recently. All that could be offered to the visitor was "bannock and cheese"!

Frank Outhwaite, of Bainbridge, used to charm me with his stories of a life that was gone — of the milking of cattle out of doors and transporting the milk to the farms in cans attached to the backs of donkeys. This was done so that the poorer land could be grazed in summer while the meadow grass grew undisturbed, to be taken as hay. Frank mentioned that Bainbridge folk had a right to put geese on Wether Fell even if they were not entitled to graze sheep there. As a child, Frank had watched flocks of geese being driven to Semerwater from Gayle or Burtersett. "When the flocks reached the skyline and saw the lake, the birds flew directly to the water." The Outhwaites, having boats on Semerwater, were often asked to help with the tricky task of rounding up the geese as summer waned.

Mrs. Mason Hodgson recalls that when she and her husband arrived at Tennant Gill, on Malham Moor, in 1938, the sheep and cattle had to compete on the grazing land with rabbits. Only 16 cattle could be kept until the rabbit problem was overcome, and then the number of cattle rose to 80. By the late 1930s, rabbit catching was not as profitable as it had been, yet the man who diligently put out snares and made regular rounds of them might catch 500 rabbits a week and earn enough to pay the rent of the farm. Rabbits had made excellent prices in the 1920s, skins being worth a shilling a time. M'duke Miller of Littondale recalled a rabbit catcher who made £400 from rabbits in one season. A fresh rabbit was a treat when a lot of meat was salted.

Eggs were preserved in a "water glass". The accent was on economy in the house. "We lived as cheaply as possible," I was told in Malhamdale. "I can remember my parents coming to Settle market and buying second-hand shoes for us. This was not a mark of poverty; it was just sensible house-keeping."

The average Dales farmer had a stoical approach to life. In a relatively good time, he would say: "Aye, but don't be rash — t'bad owd days 'll come back; they allus have done." In times of industrial depression he might comment: "We'll get through, somehow." And he would go into a state of semi-hibernation! The 1930s were a time of industrial depression and in the northern towns, cycling offered many a working man and woman a relatively cheap way of escaping from the grimy home acres into the Dales. Donald Lee, of Keighley related: "We'd go up t'Dales in an

DALES ARCHITECTURE. ABOVE: AT BARDEN, WHARFEDALE. BELOW: THE FAMOUS TAN HILL INN, NOW ON THE LINE OF THE PENNINE WAY.

hour or two. We used to take sandwiches for dinner-time and call at one of t'C.T.C. places for a pot of tea — which cost fourpence." C.T.C. was the Cyclists' Touring Club, with silver wings on its emblem.

The Browns of Cosh Farm, in the hills beyond Littondale, craved for company. The postman obligingly walked up whenever there was mail; he might otherwise have left it at Foxup. "He'd have a bite of dinner with us. If we saw some hikers passing through the farmyard, we were so pleased to see them we invited them into the house to have a cup of tea — and a chat."

In Cotterdale, I heard of the days when young men set off on bikes to attend dances that went on until 2 a.m. They hoped to be home before their fathers rose from their beds and discovered that they had been "raking about" for half the night. A lad who returned from a village "hop" with little time to spare would slip between the blankets, still wearing his clothes. Bikes were used by young men who crossed the Buttertubs Pass to dances at Keld and Muker. In due course, some of the lads clubbed together to hire a car. The charge was "ten bob a night."

Improved transport, especially motor cars, enabled some of the West Riding businessmen to move into adjacent areas of the Dales and commute daily to work. Venturesome motorists reached some outlandish places. When the "wireless" had considerable novelty value, an aura of romance lay about *Tan Hill*, England's highest hostelry and about Susan Peacock, the indomitable landlady. She and the Keld Singers featured in broadcasts from Leeds. Curiosity led hundreds of people to look for *Tan Hill*. Susan was not attracted to the wireless and her husband, Michael was "not struck wi' it either." A London visitor wrote in the visitors' book for 1935: "Broadcasting now has made 'Tan Hill' famous all England o'er, so what a joy to find it still as simple as before." A newspaper reported: "Even her experience as a radio 'star' has not robbed the hostess, Mrs. Susan Peacock, of her simple homeliness and transparent sincerity. She is not the picturesque and romantic person which many townspeople who heard her broadcast, last week, imagine her to be. The isolation of the inn is really only in a geographical sense and the scores of motorists who visit Tan Hill on Sundays create a constant link between the inn and the rest of the world."

Susan underplayed the hardship of Pennine life. She must have winced at some of the highly-coloured stories that were printed in the newspapers. In 1935, a reporter who spent an hour or two at Tan Hill recorded that a man who was leading a stallion from Whitaside to Bowes was in need of refreshments, "a request which set Mrs. Peacock frying ham and brewing tea." Then a hiker, en route from Hawes to Bowes, halted for rest and a thirst-quencher. Someone on a motor-bike arrived from the Teesdale side. "All in the middle of Mrs. Peacock's baking day!"

Susan Peacock had to make do with oil lamps. The 1930s saw the introduction of electricity to many Dales villages. One of many examples of the ingenuity shown was Jim Ward's purchase of the waterwheel from the "flagworks" at Helwith Bridge for use in generating electricity for a few properties at Horton-in Ribblesdale. At Clapham, in 1935, as already related, the Settle Electricity Company was supplying power for a penny a unit. The village had a pioneering system of electrical generation. The Farrers, having dammed up Clapdale to create Ingleborough Lake, later used a turbine to generate electricity for selected buildings, including those at the nearby woodyard, and for street lighting. I lodged with the Shaw family at the Woodyard Cottage, where an evening ritual was "switching on the street lights".

It was in the early 1930s that electricity arrived in Malhamdale. To justify the expense of wiring-up homes at the dalehead, the electricity company specified that they would only begin the work if 12 local people would subscribe. John Geldard recalled for me the struggle to get those 12 subscribers. "The general re-action was that 'we'll see how them goes on 'at gets it!' My

Raygill Farm, in Garsdale, is one of many possible examples of the unpretentious architecture of Dales farmsteads, which have been fashioned from local stone and, in this case, have been whitewashed, signifying pride of ownership. The farmer, George Metcalfe, is shown standing in a garden which has some flowers as well as vegetables. The floral appeal is largely created by lupins, once a common adornment to Dales gardens.

For every outstanding farmhouse, such as Friars Head at Winterburn, of 16th century date, there are hundreds of comparatively plain houses. Many of them date from the latter part of the 17th century. They replaced more modest structures that were usually thatched. The oldest farmsteads are where the landscape offered shelter from the worst of the weather and a good supply of fresh water by way of a beck.

parents were among the original 12 but they had electricity installed downstairs only. Four lights! They still went to bed with candles! In those days, when there was hand-milking of cows, farmers got out of bed at half-past six. I remember coming downstairs to find that my mother had the candle lit downstairs. She was frightened to put the 'lectric' on because of the expense . . ."

An electrician told us of the wonderment that showed on the faces of old folk when electricity arrived. He called at a cottage when he noticed the lights burning on a bright afternoon. The owner exclaimed: "I like 'lectric; and doesn't it last a long time?" One consumer complained: "They put t'electric in little glass bottles and you can't turn it down or blow it out."

Few Dales farms are without electricity, though supplies came so recently that older people still comment on the galaxy of bright lights on the side of a dale. Rupert Hart-Davis, who spent holidays at a cottage high on Kisdon, in upper Swaledale, writes somewhere of the fact that only two electric lights could be seen from his property, and one light was in the telephone box at Keld. In 1988, when visiting one of the remote old farms on Malham Moor, I noticed that power was being generated by a diesel engine, which was switched off when not needed.

In 1952, *The Dalesman* carried my article on T'Battery Man. It related to George Newsholme of Clapham, who was delivering batteries to the folk of the western Dales, keeping the voices

CAPON HALL, ON MALHAM MOOR, PRESIDES OVER A TRACT OF LIMESTONE COUNTRY SITUATED AT OVER 1,000 FEET ABOVE SEA LEVEL.

and music of the wireless strong and clear in cottages and farmsteads well away from electricity supplies. We travelled by a van belonging to the Craven Wireless and Electrical Service. Behind us were rows of wet batteries. George took freshly-charged batteries into the homes and returned with the "flat" batteries, being careful to attach a piece of paper to the old ones for identity. George's firm made wireless sets at a small workshop in Clapham; he had installed wirelesses at Cam and Cosh — two remote Dales farms — and he knew of a wireless at Keasden which dated back to the late 1920s. It fascinated me to hear comments about batteries. An old man in the Sedbergh area said: "Voice hes gan off t'wireless". A lady near Dent asserted: "Oh, it's thee, is it? Ah doesn't want a battery 'at leaks. Last 'un tha left leaked all ower. It maks such a blooming mess . . ."

Who could have foreseen the return to popularity of the humble goat? It was relatively common in the 1930s. Farmers kept goats to provide a supply of highly nutritious milk for needy lambs. (The goats produced their kids quite early in the year, so the milk was flowing at lambing time). Rob Hird, whose family farmed at Newby Cote, near Ingleton, has told me of goats that wandered off to the limestone crags at the head of Clapdale. Rob usually groaned when he was asked to collect the goats, for they enjoyed their freedom and rounding them up was difficult, if not hazardous. At least one animal would take to a ledge in Trow Gill. John Geldard, who farmed for many years at Malham, mentions the way that nimble goats outwitted men and dogs at Malham Cove or Gordale Scar. Over a score of goats wandered in this area.

Bill Alderson (Bill Upsteps), of Angram in Swaledale, and the young lady who became his wife, travelled from Bill's home to Tan Hill Inn on a motor bike in the days when Susan Peacock was the landlady. Susan kept a few goats to provide fresh milk for the household and guests. Bill was approached by an "auld goat" just as he was taking a packet of cigarettes from his pocket. He gave a cigarette to the goat, which swallowed it with great "relish". A pipe-smoker who was standing nearby cut a two-inch long piece from his twist tobacco, which was hard and dark, and offered this to the goat. The goat ate the twist. The two men, much amused, wondered if the next quantity of goat milk at Tan Hill would have a tobacco flavour!

With regard to the 1980s, goat milk cheese is made at Ashes Farm, North Ribblesdale. The farming couple thus make a living from 3½ acres of land, which would not be possible using sheep or cattle. The goats are milked with a machine fitted with a goat "cluster" and the best nannies give one and a half gallons of milk a day.

ON A DALES FARM

THE TERM "acre" means little to the upland farmer. For example, the parish of Chapel-le-Dale contains over 10,000 acres, but bog and outcropping rock account for a substantial area. A hill sheep does not grow fat on a limestone pavement. I was told locally: "It's curlew country. Upland. White bent [coarse grass] and rushes. We mak the best of what we have." His neighbour had remarked: "We've part stone that doesn't knaw if its limestone or sandstone; it's that queer in-between stuff." In an upland valley like Walden, the sheep and lambs are in the meadows until well into May, so the farmer does not expect to see a flush of grass until June. One farmer used to remark that "grass doesn't start growing till July, and it gives up growing in August."

The Dales farming year ran its unvarying and periodically busy course. Its highlights were tupping, lambing, peat-cutting, sheep-clipping, haytime, rush-gathering and pig-killing. I heard in Swaledale of a man who "had about 60 acre, some ewes on t'moor and two or three cows to milk. He'd sell a bit o' butter. Guys from Muker would buy that butter an' shift it." Guys also took "a few eggs". Such a man would sell two or three cows — "new-calved 'uns" — in spring. "Then he had to wait for his sheep to mak some 'brass' at back-end." Laurie Rukin told me that his father, in 1931 or 1932, took "twenty of our best wether lambs to Kirkby Stephen and I think they were six shillings each. Our half-bred lambs were sold for 14 shillings at Hawes. A good ewe brought in £1. So you couldn't go so far, could you?"

John Fothergill, who was reared in Cotterdale, recalled that in the 1930s an average Dales farm could be rented for between £50 and £60 a year. Major J.E.E. Yorke mentioned that at Halton Place, in Craven, when the early post-war boom had gone and economic conditions were very bad, he took on a farm man, who had a wife and two children. They had previously been paid 28s, plus the tenancy of a house. Major Yorke once heard an old Dales shepherd recall the days when his father died and mother had to bring up five children. The shepherd had said, simply: "We were hungered". It was a hard time for farm men. "They had no set number of hours. There were no day's off: it was a seven-day-a-week job. I remember a man working at Kirkby Top farm, in Malhamdale, in the late 1920s. The men were hired for the year then, on the first of March. He said he was not going to stop at the farm — unless the farmer paid him £1 a week."

What the old-style farmer would notice first, could he return to his native dale, would be the improvement to the meadowland through ploughing, re-seeding with a ryegrass "mix" and liberal applications of artificial fertilisers. The long established meadows and pastures were treated with lime and basic slag, in addition to the ordinary "muck", and therefore the vegetation was not under pressure. "We didn't force things to grow; nature took her own slow and quiet pace. 'Muck' was a real food for grassland and its effects lasted well." The sward was colourful, botanically rich — or "herby", to use an old term. Yorkshire fog-grass imparted an attractive smell — the well-remembered smell of new-mown hay.

Haytime has changed in recent years. It tends to be earlier. "They used to start haytime when

Beef cattle — known as sucklers — returned to many Pennine hill farms with the decline in dairy farming. The Norse folk of 1,000 and more years ago kept cattle which were driven from the winter homes to the hills in summer to take advantage of the rapid flush of vegetation induced by the summer sun.

At one time, a farmer prided himself on keeping a specific breed of cattle. Now it is a matter of so much protein on the hoof and mixed breeding is commonplace. The animals portrayed here were in a field "back o' Penyghent".

One of the most celebrated upland grazings was the 600-acre Great Close on Malham Moor where, in the 18th century, a Skipton grazier named Birtwhistle displayed cattle brought down from Scotland on the old drove roads. After being summered in Craven, cattle were driven to satisfy the craving for fresh meat on the part of the folk in the fast-growing towns.

t'sheep had been clipped; now they clip a few, make the hay, and finish off the clipping." New techniques are applied as they become available. Hay was once moved by horse-drawn sled; then they used to lead out of "pikes", which were mini-haystacks, scattered about the field, capable of being easily and quickly made in "chancy" weather, which the Pennine summer often provides. In Swaledale, an old man told me of the labour-intensive haytimes of his youth. "Grass was mown by horse-drawn machine. Then it was all done by hand-rake, strawed out, then turned, turned again and 'cocked up': then came a week o' wet weather. It had all got to be done again. Haytime was blood, sweat and tears."

At the start of haytime, the farmer went up to the top pasture where the pony had languished since muck-spreading time. He took her some Indian corn in "t'bucket bottom" and put a halter on her before leading her down to the farm to be harnessed to a mowing machine. With a double-mower, the experienced pony occupied the "grass side" and guided a younger animal through the operation. When a meadow had been cleared of hay, the ponies were quartered here for the night; they dined on the unmown strip of grass against the walls.

A Dales outbarn was wonderfully adapted to local conditions — to that fellside culture that lasted until a decline in the labour force and the coming of large-scale mechanisation. Each little barn had a shippon, with tying up for half a dozen beasts. Hay was stored in the "moo" (mow) and hay that "worn't fit to go into t'moo" was laid on baulks, above the shippon, where "it wouldn't fire."

The upper Dales, with their steep land and small fields, was horse-and-sled country. The sledges in Cowgill parish, north of Whernside, were made locally by such as Bobby Middleton. Dales joiners were supremely indifferent to their status as craftsmen and one man, when I asked him about a sledge, said: "It were nobbut a gate on its side!" Loading a sledge was a skilful occupation. A layer composed of six "kemmins" formed a "round" and three rounds were taken on and roped tightly for transportation to the barn. I asked about the art of operating a sledge, to be told: "The main job was to stick to t'horse!" My old friend Jonty Wilson, of Kirkby Lonsdale, used to spend his summer holidays at a farm near Ribblehead. He was put in charge of a Dales pony, which was attached to a sled. Said the farmer: "Thou mun go steady wi' t'hoss and sled up to t'barn. We don't want hay spilled all ower t'place." The farmer paused, then added: "But gallop back . . ."

Irishmen — the July Barbers — helped out with the hay harvest. At Tennant Gill, on Malham Moor, in 1939, an Irishman was paid £5 or £6 for a month's labour. Food and lodgings were provided. Many a Dales farmer, when questioned about the Irish labour, and asked where the Irishmen had their homes, mentioned County Mayo. After I had given a talk about everyday life in the Dales between 1900 and 1935, the woman who presided said she was descended from an old Mayo family. This led me to visit Ireland, especially Achill Isle, where inquiries confirmed that in times of economic stringency the menfolk left to help out in the rural areas of England, beginning with haytiming in the west and moving eastwards to help with the root crops.

Haytime helpers were particularly numerous before the 1914–18 war; they continued, on a dwindling scale, until the mid-1950s, by which time the Dales farms were almost fully mechanised. The Bentham hiring on June 22 saw the arrival of men who had come off the Irish boat at Heysham. They hired for a month. Then it was the turn of Hawes, in the upper Dales. Many a man did not stand around waiting to be hired; he already had a place, where he had doubtless worked in previous summers. Generations of an Irish family might go to the same farm, where they were friends of the family.

Some Irishmen preferred to fork at the forking holes; others were good at loading sledges.

One farmer discovered that he had a champion whisky distiller on his staff. Henceforth, this man was spared many of the haytime jobs. He was provided with what he needed to make whisky and told to get on with it! It is recalled that Bob o' Cam (Cam Houses, at the head of the Wharfe valley) had two or three Irishmen one year, and he bought plenty of beer — eight 16-gallon barrels of ale which cost him "six bob a barrel." Said Bob o' Cam, wonderingly — for the price asked by a merchant had been very low — "it's cheaper na tea."

The Irishmen were, by and large, very religious. Sunday morning saw them emerging from their quarters, dressed in their best clothes, and striding off down the road to the nearest Catholic churches. "The better end of the Irishmen looked very smart when they went to church. They were good citizens. Brown boots, blue suit, white shirt, smart tie, cap — always a cap . . . By Sunday night, it was generally a merry night again."

Machines took the place of the casual labourers. In the 1950s, the "pike bogey" was introduced to shift the pikes. The tractor had become commonplace. Soon, the baling machine was operating, consuming the rows of hay and regurgitating them as compact bales. (In winter, the twine cut from the bales became the farmer's best friend, being used for a variety of jobs, even the repair of gates and as emergency braces for his trousers!").

Farmers worked ceaselessly to keep the landscape tidy. John Geldard remembers when all Cove pastures at Malham were covered with bracken. "Willie Hudson eradicated that by mowing them twice a year — by scythe. If I saw four men up there, mowing away with scythes, I'd go and help them because bracken was useful as bedding. So were rushes. It was all very economical. I've been on to Settle tops mowing rushes for bedding in the days when Mr. Pattinson farmed at Scosthrop Hall. You had to have a sharp scythe when you were mowing rushes. It was hard work. It made you sweat, but the rushes cost nothing. Farmers didn't buy straw as they do nowadays. You see wagons full of straw coming into the Dales by the dozen."

The period just after the 1939–45 war was the start of more prosperous times for farmers. The value of stock had risen appreciably and a farmer was getting a better income. "They had all got on to milk selling; they all had a better income and it was beginning to show. Following heavy sheep losses in bad winters, the government introduced a hill sheep subsidy. This subsidy and other grants were to be the salvation of hill farmers.

The Dales landscape began to change considerably as an effort was made to improve hill land by gripping [mechanical drainage]. The fells, which used to act as a giant sponge, retaining the water that fell as rain and releasing it gradually, began to part with the water in savage, peat-ridden spates. There has been a natural erosion, through hot sun, drying winds and heavy rain, of the once extensive areas of blanket peat. Old meadowland was ripped up by tractors, re-seeded with strains of grass suitable for silage-making and fed mighty doses of "artificials" to produce bumper crops for the bumper herds. They now extend, sappy and green, from horizon to horizon, nurtured by what has been called "Bank till". The modern fertilisers force the growth of grass to sustain the huge modern herds of cattle.

Such changes have been disastrous to wildlife. For example, the partridge thrived in the pre-war period — that is, before the ploughing out of vast areas of rough, ill-drained ground which favoured a variety of bird life. Today, when silage grass is cut twice a year, the partridge rarely has a chance to raise a brood. I know an area of rough, scrubby ground where a few partridges remain. In dry weather, I see them dust-bathing beside the road. One year I stood beside a newly-hatched brood and waved down speeding vehicles so that the tiny chicks, in their mottled down, would not be flattened against the tarmac. Partridge chicks are among the most dainty of young birds.

In the 1930s, a sheep was not ill for long. As a Dales farmer told me: "It awther got better — or deed." This was the period when medicine came out of a bottle — and if the farmer was feeling under the weather he might surreptitiously have a swig! A goat was tethered in the shippon where a cow was inclined to abort its calf.

Our photograph [by Bertram Unne] shows an ailing sheep being brought back to the farm on a horse-drawn sled. Many Dales farmers in the period of industrial depression could not afford the services of a vet.

James Herriot, author of the delightful books about a vet's life in the Dales, recalls that when he was married in the 1930s, the honeymoon was spent at "The Wheatsheaf" at Carperby, in Wensleydale. Having little money, and with some of the veterinary work overdue, that honeymoon was largely spent tuberculin testing cattle!

LEARNING THE CRAFT OF DRYSTONE WALLING AT SEDBUSK, WENSLEYDALE.

Now, the threat is from a farm tractor with machine in tow. An old friend remarks: "Chaps can't help it. Tractors go at such a speed! When there were horses doing the haulage work in a hayfield, a farmer would rein the horse in if he saw a bird fluttering ahead and either avoid a nest or chase the young birds away." Speedy and ruthless farm operations have thinned out the hare population and the first cut for silage often finds the young of the curlew half grown and incapable of flight. The Dales used to be alive with lapwings — known to the dalesman as "tewits". Now you may see half a dozen in a year. A sporting man commented about the partridge: "If you go into a field with a covey in it, there are probably up to 100 cows grazing. You daren't shoot . . ."

The modern substitute for a wall is post and wire, in the use of which a Dales farmer might even be grant-aided. Some good wallers remain. You see them working in friendly competition at agricultural shows such as Kilnsey, where the Crag forms an impressive backdrop. The Young Farmers' Clubs have encouraged walling, and — happily — the highway authority has frequently built walls in the traditional way as part of road improvement schemes. For example, five miles of drystone walling mark the boundaries of the Settle by-pass (1987–88).

A Dales wall is really two walls in one, side by side. The two sections are held together by "throughs" and small stones form the packing. Wallers are accustomed to working with a variety of material, from the water-smoothed "cobbles" from a beck to stones with an "edge" in gritstone areas. (Notice the neat wall across the summit of Whernside). A wall-top consists of a protective line of capstones. Such a wall, if properly made, will last a century or more. It provides "bield" [shelter] for sheep which, standing in the lee, are kept dry. A wall is useful to wild life, offering a perch to the wheatear and a nesting site to the pied wagtail. I have found a crow nest on a wall and a blackbird nest in a cavity under a capstone.

If a gap occurs, the material for repair is readily to hand. For a time, the wall might be "singled" to prevent stock from straying. In due course, the gap-waller arrives. The tumbled stone is cleared and the foundation of the gapped area dug out afresh. A typical Dales wall is four feet wide at the bottom, tapering to two and a-half feet, this tapering being known as the "batter". Old wallers have told me about the necessity to cross joints, to have plenty of good "throughs" and to leave no large spaces between stones. By deliberate plan, many walls incorporate a "cripple-oil" or creep, which permits mixed-grazing. The cows are held in a selected field and the much smaller sheep may pass from one field to another. When not needed, a creep is blocked by a single large flat stone.

An early conversation I had with a waller took place in upper Wharfedale in 1952. Tommy Chapman, of Buckden, a farm man, spent a good half of his time piecing together the jig-saw puzzle that is a Dales stone wall. He was taught the craft by Albert Mitton, of Buckden. Tommy had heard that most of the walls around Buckden were erected as part-time work by the lead miners, who were paid about a shilling a day. "A lot of farmers don't seem to take time with the walls. They just throw them up any way. And, of course, there's not the labour there used to be". (These words were spoken 36 years ago!) "If you put a wall up right, it should easily last a lifetime. You get a real thrill in making a good wall. No two stones are alike, so the work is never monotonous. Today we don't put in the hours we used to do. I started at eight in the morning and walled away until ten at night!"

ROADSIDE SENTRY IN THE DAYS BEFORE CATTLE GRIDS WERE COMMON.

CATTLE AND SHEEP

KIT CALVERT of Wensleydale became a farmer in the Depression Years of the early 1930s. "There'd been something of a slump in trade, but in 1931 we had an idea that it had touched the bottom. Trade was bound to improve!" Kit's farm was "unhandy", made up of parcels of land. He paid £70 a year rent for 25 acres of meadow and about the same area of inland pastures. There were also two old pastures on Wether Fell. "I was getting only 5d a gallon for my milk in summer and 8d in winter. We did retail a bit ower t'counter to regular customers, and that brought in a bit more brass." In 1928, his top lambs made £2 each; in the second year it was 30s and in 1930 the price was 17s 3d. "The last lot of lambs I sold was the best I had ever reared."

In 1933, Kit met a farmer whose unfriendly bank manager had left him without a penny. Kit arranged to take some lambs to the mart but not to sell them; he would simply get a valuation. "I then arranged that the destitute farmer would slaughter off the lambs, one at a time, and would hawk the meat in a basket. Anything he made over the valuation price, which was 16s a lamb, would be split between us."

At that time, the Dales farmer was dependent on the textile areas and the Durham coalfield as markets for his produce. Life in the towns was even more desperate than it was in the country. Kit remembered being driven through a number of colliery villages, where shops were boarded up and the men who sat or crouched round the war memorial looked pinched, starved and grey.

Some Dales farmers were declared bankrupt; others committed suicide, but most of them survived in a fashion. Kit Calvert travelled over the Buttertubs Pass, into Swaledale, to buy bankrupt stock. He bought ewes at 5s 6d each and an old tup for 7s 6d, also hens at 9d each, with a small hen hut "thrown in". Two lads who assisted Kit to drive the stock back to Wensleydale were delighted when he gave them the hens and the hut. Another time, he bought a useful little cow for £14 15s and he kept her for five years. When Kit took over the management of the Creamery at Hawes, he left the cow with his brother Bob and she continued to have calves. In 1936, Bob told Kit that the "old lady" was finished; she had not wintered well, but was holding yet another calf. Kit gave the cow to his brother, who drove her to market, but was "shamed" because the cow looked so run-down. John Drinkall, the cattle dealer, was looking for cheap stock. He paid £26 10s for her!

The Dales farmer of the 1930s did not attend auction marts much and was at the mercy of the dealer. A man who toured Malhamdale asking the farmers if they had any geld cows — anything, indeed, to sell — became a wealthy man. He left £20,000 or so, which was considered by his friends and neighbours to be "a lot o' brass". Such men were welcome at the farms because the farmers themselves did not have the facilities for taking stock to market. Laurie Rukin's father took a geld cow to Hawes in 1932. Tom Milner was one of the auctioneers. Father asked how much the cow had brought and was told £12. He said: "I can't get a new suit for that." Another Shorthorn, "a dark-roaned 'un which won first prize", brought £22 10s. The following week he had a light-roaned cow that won second prize and was sold for £21.

FRED TAYLOR IN THE SMALL MUSEUM ESTABLISHED AT WEST MARTON DAIRY.

In the 1930s, the Shorthorn cow graced almost every Dales pasture. Another "coloured" beast was the gentle Ayrshire. Today, the milk cattle are Friesians, which — in the early days of the breed's introduction — were known to an old Swaledale friend as "watter-cans"! A few Shorthorns remained, and in the summer of 1979 I had the unexpected treat of seeing a herd of over 100 animals being kept on West Park, near Cotherstone, by Thomas Birkett, a founder of the Northern Dairy Shorthorn Breeders' Society. He could not bear to part with them when his neighbours went over to the Freisian breed. Thomas remained steadfastly old-fashioned and none of his cattle was de-horned, the fashion since the 1950s. Incidentally, there used to be a debate in the Dales about the form the horns should take, up or down. An old farmer listened to the talk and then demolished the argument by remarking: "It doesn't matter. You don't get milk out of the horns."

At Thomas Birkett's farm, it was a memorable experience to walk through large, well-drained fields and see Shorthorns kept in the traditional way. The milk cows were handy to the byre and dried-off cows grazed in the next field. Beyond that was a field of bullocks. I walked to the edge of the moor and noted that in the last good field, just short of the moorland grazings, were the in-calf heifers and stirks. The youngest stock occupied a large pasture near the farm. Inside the buildings was the latest crop of calves and a sturdy Shorthorn bull. This remarkable survival of the old Dales way of life was auctioned in September, 1979.

Fred Taylor, who was reared at Dent, has recalled when the price of farmhouse butter was as low as 6d a pound. That period saw the growth of liquid milk sales from the farms. The Milk Marketing Board was formed in 1933. At a slightly earlier period, Frank Dinsdale of Dent had become "the saviour of the dale" because he collected surplus milk and made it into cheese. "We made butter till Frank started collecting at sixpence a gallon." The factory production of cheese in Wensleydale had begun under Edward Chapman as early as 1897. When the dairies at Hawes and Askrigg were temporarily in difficulty, the Guys of Swaledale sent some of their cheese to the Co-op in Middleton-in-Teesdale, receiving 4½d a pound for it when trade was at its most depressed state.

Until the 1930s, most Dales farms churned the milk and used the cream for butter-making. Butter was generally retailed in quite small pats, but if a large slab of butter was required, it was laid on a butter-worker so that the moisture was removed effectively. Settle was known as a market at which good butter was sold. I heard from a North Ribblesdale woman: "It was pitiful to see the farmers' wives standing in a row and to notice that one poor woman had been left with her butter till last. She'd be shamefaced, yet the poor quality of her butter might be nothing to do with her skill and care — it was simply that the land on which the cattle grazed was poor."

Dick Guy, of Swaledale, bought butter in the upper dale and transported it across the Buttertubs Pass to Hawes, where much of it was sold "to a chap from Nelson. He made sweets. He bought butter for as little as 5d a pound." John Willie Heseltine travelled to Hawes market from his home in West Burton. He bought butter and sold it in Northallerton. "He didn't bother with Hawes if he'd got plenty o' butter from the folk in Bishopdale."

The state of the soil and the "herb of the land" were prime factors in the production of good cheese. In pre-factory days, Dalesfolk poured the night's milk into a large copper cheese kettle that was kept warm for the souring process to take place. The morning's milk might be added to that already in the "kettle". Some people made the cheese in the kettle. Rennet was stirred in, and then the curds were cut, stirred, the whey drained away and the curds put in a special bag that was hung up to allow more whey to drain off. Towards night, some salt was added, the quantity depending on the size of the cheese it was proposed to make. Wensleydale cheeses were

Left: Kit Calvert, of Hawes, complete with clay pipe, presided over the Creamery for many years.

Right: Testing Wensleydale cheese. It is the generic name for cheese made in the dale and adjacent valleys.

made up to 10lb in weight.

It was a firm idea that in cheese-making, all the moisture should be removed — hence the popularity of enormous stone presses. This proved to be fallacious. The metal presses that subsequently appeared in the Dales had long metal arms, on which weights could be placed to maintain constant pressure on the cheese during the many hours it remained in the press. In Dentdale, a wooden cheese mould was used, the curds being wrapped in muslin. In Craven, these moulds were like huge cake tins pitted with holes. A cheese removed from the press was bandaged and laid on a shelf in the "cheese house", being turned daily for about 10 days as it dried. Such cheese was left for several weeks to ripen prior to use. A cheese that was to have a mould was stored low down, where the humidity was at its highest, and cheeses that were to be dried fairly quickly were placed on the higher shelves. When Frank Dinsdale was cheese-making at Sedbergh, one buyer would say: "I'll tak every cheese that has a fur coat on it." So they selected cheese with a mould about an inch long. "That man knew it would be a lively cheese."

The Guys of Hill Top, Swaledale, milked about 14 cows and had a daily output of three or four cheeses in the main season. Huge stone cheese presses stood out of doors and were used when it was necessary to remove most of the whey so that the cheeses would keep for the winter. J.R. Guy, early this century, rose from his bed at 3.30 a.m. when it was market day at Barnard Castle. He took cheeses to market fortnightly, usually having between 20 and 30 large cheeses for sale, most of them being bought for the miners of County Durham.

In 1912, the enterprising Alfred Rowntree converted an inn, *The Lady Babs*, into a creamery. (This being Coverdale, my Lady Babs was a racehorse!). The enterprising Alfred had piggeries constructed. He fed the animals on whey and any surplus "blue" milk [what was left when the cream had been skimmed from it]. For years, the "cheese factory" at Coverdale was owned by "Cow and Gate", and during the war traditional type Cheddar and Cheshire cheeses were produced. Then, under the Milk Marketing Board, Wensleydale cheese became the chief product.

The activities of the Dinsdale brothers — Frank, Eddie and John — at their Dent creamery, were applauded by the farm folk. The brothers hailed from Wensleydale; they kept the village shop at Dent and also had a farm. When they began collecting milk from the other farms, they provided each with a gallon measure. Milk was collected in 17 gallon churns (kits) and a small van was bought to extend the service to Garsdale. The Dinsdales began with a vat of 50 gallon capacity. It was a "jacketed" affair, allowing for a flow of heated water around it. The capacity was later extended to over 200 gallons, and in due course the activity shifted to Farfield Mill at Sedbergh, where some 3,000 pounds of cheese a day were produced. Farmers approached Frank Dinsdale for cheeses to be used at haytime. He made the cheeses in May or early June, as the cows were being turned out and the milk was rich. Fred Taylor relates: "If a farmer wanted a 10-pounder, we used to knock off the value of 10 gallons of milk, and the cheese-maker expected that a bob would be put into his pocket."

It is now a rare privilege to watch Dales cheese being made in a farmhouse. Marjorie Longstaff was still making the Swaledale variety at Deer Park, Harkerside, high above the river, when I called there in 1985. A narrow gate set in a roadside wall gave access to a field path through an old-established pasture where ploughshares had not been used. The land was unfertilised other than by "muck", the traditional Pennine pick-me-up for jaded acres. At Deer Park the pasture held Tiny, an eight-year-old red Shorthorn with a crumpled horn, and Blackie, a matronly Friesian. It was their milk that had gone into the cheese. Mrs. Longstaff offered me a wedge-shaped piece. The cheese lingered on my tongue, melting in my mouth, imparting a mellow herby flavour.

FARMHOUSE CHEESE-MAKING EQUIPMENT IN THE WEST MARTON MUSEUM.

The use of the term "Swaledale" cheese by the cheese-makers of Swaledale reflects the pride they feel in the native valley. Swaledale cheese is still being produced as such, though most Dalesfolk would use "Wensleydale cheese" as the generic name. Marjorie Longstaff, who retired to nearby Reeth, had been fortunate in being able to watch her mother make cheese at Blea House. In mother's time, many of the cows were being milked by hand in remote pastures, so that the meadows could be kept clear of stock and therefore untrampled in the weeks before haytime. The milk from the cattle was conveyed to the farm by back-can.

New-calved cows were always cheap to buy in spring because when cows went out to grass there was a large increase in the amount of milk they produced. A farmer did not need to buy additional cattle at that time. In the autumn, however, the amount of milk per cow fell and it was the best time to sell cows. "When it got to November", I was told, "store cattle were bad to sell because it was getting to the time when they were going to be put inside. If it had been a bad summer, with a poor hay crop, nobody wanted them. They were disposed of at give-away prices."

When milk production began in the Dales, a balanced dairy ration was available for high production. There was a choice of a good quality feed or you could have a balanced dairy cake. "That was quite an improvement on the 1920s when there were only two sorts of cattle cake — linseed slab cake and cotton cake. You had to break up the slabs of cake with a hammer and then put it over into the booses for the cows to eat. I've seen a neighbour and his man carrying these long slabs of cake from the farm to an outbarn, nearly a mile away. Each man had one of these things under each arm." The story was told of a "proven" merchant who went to Capon Hall, on Malham Moor, in the hope of selling some cake. "He had a job to persuade the farmer to buy any, and eventually the farmer decided to get half a hundredweight 'and see how I go on wi' it.' Perhaps he expected some wonderful results from that half hundredweight, for when the traveller returned he said, testily: "Well I've used your cake but I haven't noticed any difference.'"

Tuberculosis was prevalent in the 1930s. "I remember my father having a case in his little herd. The Ministry gave him three-quarters of the animal's value when he destroyed it. The object was eradication of the disease. The next scheme was for the testing of all the herds. It took a lot of years but eventually it was gone. Any reactors had to be sold. They compensated the farmer, of course."

Nearly every farmer kept two or three pigs. The breed was mainly Large White and piglets were to be bought from one of the many local pig-breeders. "It was all to do with economical living," says a farmer from Malhamdale.

If a farmer sold a calf that was not many days old, he tied it up in sacking, with only its head protruding, when he wished to transport it to another farm or to market. One of the sadnesses of my young life was to see such a calf on a platform at Skipton railway station. I once asked about this, to be told that it was quite comfortable really and the sacking helped to keep it warm. The old-time farmer did not keep a calf long because he wanted the cow's milk for sale or butter-making. The sooner he got rid of his unwanted bull calves, the better. The RSPCA waged a successful campaign to abolish the movement of calves of such tender age. In any case, some farmers began to deal in calves, touring the Dales to buy them at about 15s each.

When Artificial Insemination was introduced, the milk yield was improved enormously. It had got to do — to pay for the cow and for the tillage. And the rent, of course . . . Now almost every cow you see in the Dales is a Friesian. "You used to have those nice sleek Shorthorns and Ayrshires. Now you hardly ever see a coloured cow. They're black-and-white. We didn't like the

A CLAPHAM FARMER TAKES PRIDE IN REMOVING THE LAST OF THE RAKINGS (photo: E.C. Morris).

HAND-RAKING IN A MEADOW AT RAINSCAR, BACK O' PENYGHENT.

changeover at the time, but now we're used to it. A different type of cow gives a much improved yield as a result of the AI." A Walden farmer observed: "I think the biggest switch during the last 10 years has been that from milk production to stock-rearing and beef production . . . We seem to keep everything 'cept goats."

In the 1930s, the system of stocking was to divide the acreage by three and multiply it by two. That was the number of sheep it would carry. "They don't stick to that now."

The Dales country reeks with sheep. Tending them was once left to a full-time shepherd who was paid — and not very well — by those who had grazing rights. John Scarr, one of four shepherds on Abbotside Common, above Wensleydale, in the early 1930s, was paid £2 a week for his pains. "You had yourself and your dogs to keep from that wage," he told me. In Nidderdale, the estate employed a shepherd for Ramsgill and Heathfield, but at Stean the land was "stinted", a stint representing the pasturage of a sheep. The local farmers who had stints met to appoint a shepherd to look after their interests. A man who attended a meeting noticed with what keenness they fixed a price. "They didn't half grind him down." Thomas Joy, of Grassington, saw the job of shepherd on Grassington Moor advertised in 1940 and, putting in a modest bid, was given the job at 38s a week. He worked more by the calendar than the clock. "The weather ruled." In hard weather, he would reach the edge of the Moor to find up to 700 sheep congregating on this low ground. He would drive them higher, anxious that they should not puddle up a limited area, but "they stayed about the area and then crept back again."

Just before clipping time came the washing of the sheep in a beck which had been "demmed" with stones and sods to create a sizeable pool. About 1,000 sheep were gathered and brought down to the nearby fold, from which each animal was manhandled to the pool. Two men took one sheep, one man grabbing the breast and the other the buttocks, and then deftly turned the animal upside down before tossing it into the water, from which it swam as best it could. True washing, or "dollying", was in an earlier period. At that time, a serious attempt was made to wash the underparts of each sheep.

In Kingsdale, near Ingleton, Edward Batty told me of the sheep complaint which farmers called moss illness, staggers or tremblings. It was later known to be caused by a calcium deficiency. Before that discovery was made, in about 1930, there was no effective remedy. Edward said: "You gave 'em summat. Odd 'uns got right. A lot died. Then, with calcium, a sheep that looked dead, or could hardly wink, was soon up on its feet again — and away!"

In humid weather there might be an infestation of maggots which, if not attended to, led to the deaths of many of the sheep. A maggot-ridden sheep was a sorry sight, and from it came a distinctive smell. Thomas Joy, working on Grassington Moor, had a dog which could easily detect such sheep through its finely-developed sense of smell. "We used to rub fine, dry peat on a sheep's skin if it was not broken; it was said to discourage the flies from striking." (This moorland shepherd, who died in 1982, had seen many strange sights, and none more curious than the sheep and lamb he found, side by side and quite dead. They had been struck simultaneously by lightning!).

Fifty years ago, when sheep were bringing from 12s to 15s, a Dales vet was rarely consulted about their well-being. If they were ill, they died or were knocked on the head by the farmer. As the price of sheep increased, so did the necessity for a vet to know about sheep ailments, because now he was being consulted more and more about them.

Money counted more than time or effort. William Brown, of Cosh, at the very head of Littondale, drove sheep for 10 miles to Hawes market. He was not averse to driving them back home again if he did not consider the price was adequate. In 1933, a time of Depression, his son

The farmer in the upper Dales spends much of the year attending to sheep. When he is not actually dipping, clipping or spaining [separating the ewes from the lambs in early autumn] he is simply looking — or leuking! The sheep-clippers (above) were operating in a field near Wainwath Falls, Swaledale. The farmer (right) had penned some sheep beside the Buttertubs Pass and was studying their form and condition.

Richard drove sheep to Hawes, confidently expecting them to realise £2 10s each. They fell short of this figure, so the sheep were walked back to Cosh. Another day they were driven to Crummack, near Austwick, and on the following day to Bentham mart. "The sheep were sold for sixpence apiece more than had been offered at Hawes! But Dad was satisfied that we'd got the best possible price."

The small-time farmer of the 1930s reared a couple of pigs. "They used to say that t'nicest pictures you had in t'house was when you had four hams and four sides hanging up . . ."

It has given me pleasure, over the years, to seek out the truly remote Dales farms and to meet families who have not been able to see another inhabited building from the windows of their homes. To visit such a farm is an adventure. To meet self-sufficient folk is to be reminded of the Dales life that was. Birkdale Farm, tucked away at the head of Teesdale, has been linked historically with Dufton parish. I once walked from Langdon Beck to Birkdale and on to High Cup Nick, descending to Dufton, and I cannot recall meeting another soul. I had the moor sheep and the moor birds for company.

The story is told of an old lady who died at Birkdale, her body being borne on the back of a pony for burial at Dufton. The funeral party tied the horse to a tree as they went into the inn for refreshments; when they emerged, they found the pony had slipped its halter and had set off back to Birkdale Farm. It is said that when it came in sight of Birkdale, the children said: "Grannie's coming back!"

When I chatted with Brian Bainbridge, tenant of Birkdale, he told me of walking his half-bred sheep to Appleby by way of the rim of High Cup Nick. I heard that the farmhouse is lit up by power from a generator and that Calor gas is used for cooking. A coal fire is the source of cheer on chill winter days. "We get coal once a year, when we sell our first lot of lambs. As soon as we have a trailer coming back empty, we start stocking up for the winter . . ."

My first view of Cam Houses, some 35 years ago, was also the best. I approached on foot, following the Devil's Highway — the old Roman road — from near Gearstones, over Cam End. Again, I had the golden plover and the sheep for company. Today, the area is the crossing point between the Pennine Way and the Dales Way. This is Two Rivers country. From Cam Houses, there is an uninterrupted view of the area that sees the source of the Greenfield Beck (flowing to the Wharfe) and Cam Beck (a tributary of the Ribble). Such is the lie of the land you would swear that in its early stages, Cam Beck is flowing uphill!

I last saw Cam Houses in the spring of 1988 when, having a date with black grouse in Greenfield Forest, I glanced across the shallow valley to where the cluster of farms looked, in the silvery morning mist, like some natural outcrop. Years ago, the place was a thriving community of several families. The families cheerfully adapted themselves to life in seclusion at an elevation above sea level of 1,450 feet. Cam Houses was the permanent home of only one family, the Middletons, who had erected a barn of breeze blocks and corrugated asbestos and were busy preparing an old building as a "bunk barn" for visitors, under a scheme devised by the Dales National Park.

The second of the two remaining farms at Cam was owned by the Beresfords, who arrived in 1931 with their possessions stacked on a horse-drawn cart. They now attend to Cam Houses from a permanent house at Newby Head, between Ingleton and Hawes. Mrs. Beresford told me of life at Cam — of laborious hand operations like butter-making, and of social occasions, such as whist drives and dances held at Oughtershaw.

What happened in winter was governed by the weather. Early in 1979, when snow was piled up around Cam in enormous drifts, the Middletons were marooned for almost the entire period

Left: Nature, by providing a sheep with substantial horns, made it comparatively easy for this Whaw (Arkengarthdale) man to control it! Above: The farmer has a number of crooks for various purposes. A lambing crook, which is longer than the average, is used for slipping round the neck of any lamb that needs attention. The crook pictured here was made for show. The owner would be a sporty person, for the carvings are of hound, fox and terrier.

This solitary farm is Newby Head. It is less remote than you might suppose, standing beside the old turnpike between Lancaster and York — a road that has been much improved and gives ready access from North Craven to Hawes. The farmer also used to provide hospitality for travellers.

Newby Head would be the area where the sheep of Newby (now in the parish of Clapham) were summered. The modern farmer has to put up signs in spring warning motorists of the presence of jay-walking lambs. Each year, a number perish under the wheels of speeding vehicles.

Newby Head is close to the old county boundary (West Riding/North Riding). Today, you pass from Craven into Richmondshire. The high land behind the farm extends to the limestone summit acres of Wold Fell, source of Gayle Beck, the longest feeder of the river Ribble. Arguably, Wold Fell is the source of the river but the originators of the Ribble Way opted for a high point on the fell opposite.

between Christmas and Easter. The Army obliged with helicopter drops of "proven" for the stock. Mrs. Middleton went shopping to Hawes, travelling on a Scorpion tank! Kit Calvert used to tell me of the days of Bob o' Cams (Bob Lambert). An intending purchaser of "owd Scotch tups" visited the remote place and found the sheep waiting for his inspection — in the parlour of Bob's house!

Another famous old Pennine farm, Hell Gill, takes its name from the gorge lying on the old Yorkshire–Westmorland border, a gorge named after the Norse "hella", meaning a cave. The old Hell Gill farmhouse has a peat store which, it was said, could accommodate 1,000 turves. You simply drove up with horse-drawn cart, backed the outfit to the side of the house and tossed the "peats" into a doorway, from which they fell a maximum distance of 25 feet.

Foxup, at the head of Littondale, is remote enough. Travel a mile-and-a-half beyond Foxup, among the quiet fells, and you come to Cosh, which like Hell Gill is no longer occupied by farm folk. Early this century, Cosh was home to the Brown family, who walked five miles to Horton-in-Ribblesdale to catch a train and would uncomplainingly drive surplus sheep for 10 miles to the market at Hawes. One December day, the snow lay at Cosh for so long there was a danger that the sheep might starve. So William Brown gathered them, mounted his pony and drove the sheep across the white landscape looking for green fields where farmers might provide grazing for a copper or two per sheep. There were 450 sheep. He spent the first night with friends at Neils Ing, "back o' Penyghent", and then he moved on towards the Ribble Valley, where William found quarters for his animals at Wigglesworth. They were allowed to stay here for a whole month and henceforth, the stock from Cosh Farm were referred to as "them snowbound sheep". Conversely, each summmer, up to 50 cattle belonging to other farmers were "gisted" at Cosh and took advantage of the flush of good sweet grass.

John Harker, who lives at Lofthouse, showed me the wood-and-metal spade with its single "wing" and initials IJ burnt on the handle. The spade had belonged to Isaac Joy, of a family long associated with the upper valley of the Nidd. When I chatted with Mr. Harker in 1984, I heard that he was the last man in the locality to lift, dry and transport peat from the local moors for burning in the domestic grate. "When I was a lad in farm service, we got a lot of 'peearts' on Stean Moor. We used a barrow. Twenty-one 'peearts' to the barrow; 21 barrows to the sledge-load." The sledge was drawn by a horse. In 1983, John Harker had taken advantage of the especially dry conditions to drive his tractor into the peat pit. "I lived at one place where they did without coal for three years; nothing but peat was burnt on the fire." He remembered when the topmost peat (turf) was cut into "hubs" and allowed to smoulder away. "They were sometimes called 'Saturday nighters' because they lasted a long time. Many a time, there would be enough red-hot ashes next morning to start of another peat fire." Mr. Harker referred to peat-cutting as "gravin" and said it was a job that began when the manure had been spread, the cattle had been turned out and the sheep were on the moor.

Twice a year, a tenant farmer prepared himself for his Day of Reckoning, otherwise known as Rent Day. In the 1930s, landlords did not go the rounds every three years putting up the rent, as they do today. In times of industrial depression, the rent might actually be reduced or even waived. In any case, "whatever a farm was let for on the open market, that figure stood until the farmer left and the place changed hands. There was no question of 'rent reviews'." A Rent Day recalled by a landowner in Ribblesdale took place at the office in his home, there being no pub in the village. Instead of a meal or a drink, a tenant was given "a bit o' luck". The bank manager was in attendance and quite often a farmer would hand over his cheque book and tell him what he should write. "Then there was a bit of gossip and we'd have a bit of a laugh."

A farmer who was known to be extremely idle — "except at using a beer glass" — made a great show of producing his wallet and a few greasy £10 notes. He'd say: "I had to sell a cow yesterday to get down here." And he would fumble in his wallet for a considerable time. "We'd get a cheque for perhaps £15 and the rest of the money in dirty notes. But that's a long time past . . ."

A tenant farmer in the 1930s usually worked very hard — for very little. Benny Taylor, agent for the Metcalfes of Ings House estate, at the head of Wensleydale, held "rent days" at the *Crown* in Hawes. When times were bad, the first farmer would moan and say that he could not pay the rent. The next, of a more jovial nature, would offer to send Benny some more later, when he had sold a cow. An optimist like Jack Chapman, who had a little farm, would say: "Well, there's nowt this quarter, Benny. I've nowt and you've nowt, so there's nowt for noan on us. Thou'll hev to git a bit of old fence pulled down. I'll put up a new fence instead of paying t'rent."

Winter deals savagely with the Pennines. The wife at a high-lying farm told me: "Every winter I seem to get another skin!" The terrible winter of 1947 began wih a normal fall of snow during January, but February opened with a blizzard that continued relentlessly until March 15. It was not the weight of snow but the ferocity of the wind that brought life to a standstill. Snow cleared from the roads during the day was blown back by night. Aircraft dropped bundles of hay to remote farms when food for the stock was exhausted. In any case, the quality of the hay that winter was poor, a consequence of a dreadful hay harvest in 1946.

Electricity had not yet reached the majority of Dales farms. The womenfolk had to cope with limited food, for wartime rationing had continued into an austere and uneasy peace. Some farmers' wives revived the old butter and cheese-making skills so that the milk which could not be cleared by road transport would not be wasted. German prisoners were drafted in to help clear the roads. It is related that on March 12, when conditions were desperate, Dick Guy ventured from Muker into the upper dale with some hay. The vehicle was locked in by a blizzard and could not be cleared for nine days. A district nurse, told of the imminent birth of a child, set out from Reeth to Ravenseat in her car, walked from Thwaite to Keld and completed the journey on ponyback.

At Vallance Lodge, head of Teesdale, the sheep population peaks at just under 3,000 and then drops for the winter to the basic stock of breeding ewes [some 1,400] and 400 hoggs [young sheep] plus the tups. The big fields, so often swept by rain or snow, contain large Y-shaped drystone structures erected for "bield" or shelter. Small circular crofts were built on the open fell. The shape is such that when the "snow dogs" are howling, snow is whirled around, leaving the croft relatively free of snow. Tales are told of the 1947 wintry spell that left 1,100 sheep dead at Vallance Farm alone. Another farmer in the dale carefully nurtured his flock of some 80 ewes the winter through, only to have them swept away when the beck came out in savage spate with the thaw.

A Walden man mentioned a February day in 1947 when he expected a delivery of coal. The merchant, noticing a few flakes of snow in the air, postponed the delivery until the following day. That night, a blizzard deposited thick snow in the dale. Little more snow fell, but a dry wind created an undulating white "desert". The dalesfolk had to stay home for weeks on end. A family without coal felled a large tree and burnt that. They had a pig for food and a horse to carry them on their limited journeys from home.

In 1962, the Bainbridges of Birkdale, at the head of Teesdale, started the winter with some 400 ewes. They were in the process of building up the flock. Snow fell, and the ground became an undulating white desert. On the clear, sunny, bitterly cold days that followed, three-quarters of the flock perished. In spring, an unnatural quietness prevailed at Birkdale. Not a sheep bleated.

More recently, snow came out of a clear sky in April. "It was a lovely day on the Thursday, but by Friday morning we got up to find it was snowing," recalled Mary Bainbridge, the farmer's wife. "By dinner-time, there was a blizzard and we couldn't see a thing." Shocked by the impact of the storm, and by the effect of some recent innoculations, the sheep decided to lamb all at once. "They were dropping lambs in the snow . . . We put them in the buildings and we had a house full of lambs. I was taking milk out of a ewe and feeding any lamb, just to keep it going. And all the time I was thinking: what if the ewes don't take to their lambs when conditions improve?" Happily, when the ewes and lambs were turned out of doors, almost all of them were re-united.

The indifferent climate, the difficulty of taking fodder to sheep on the steep flanks of the local fell and the high labour costs, leading to a low level of manning, persuaded a Chapel-le-Dale farmer to build a huge shelter of breeze blocks and Yorkshire boarding, with an asbestos roof — a structure large enough to hold 500 sheep. At the time I saw it, the building was home to some 400 expectant ewes, or half the total on this large farm, where it had been arranged for the sheep to lamb in two distinct batches.

All this was at a site where farming has been continuous since the days of the Norse settlers.

LEADING HAY FROM "PIKES" AT APPERSETT, IN WENSLEYDALE (photo: P. Walshaw).

A Year in the Dales

NO LONGER are the Dales sheep washed, as was the case when this photograph was taken at Keasden, in the parish of Clapham, where the moorland beck was dammed up, a large workforce assembled and sheep were dropped into the water to have their wool ruffled and grit and dirt from the moors swept away about a fortnight before clipping time.

It happened within living memory. Old men who attended a washing tell of the coldness of the water, in which some of them stood waist deep for hours on end; they also mention that the last trace of salve applied to the skins of the sheep in the previous autumn was washed away and, entering the water, stupified the fish, leading to some toothsome meals of fresh trout.

Though a farmer might travel about by tractor, Land Rover or vehicle with "balloon tyres", and has much better protective clothing than did his forebears, farming is still not an easy occupation. Those engaged in it have to face the ancient enemies — the often grim weather, especially the long winter, and the thin soils.

A Pennine moor is not the easiest area on which to operate. Where the heather is rank, it drags against the legs, impeding progress. In moist areas, the sphagnum moss forms bright green carpets that often conceal a treacherously soft place. The moorland peat, now being eroded by wind and weather, forms hillocks that are moist and brown. Add to this the mist and the rain . . .

The mounted farmer in our photograph was operating on the Teesdale side of The Stang. His pony not only saved his legs but enabled him to see further. The Dales pony is still bred and displayed at annual shows in Teesdale and adjacent valleys. It has been described as a miniature cart horse and was once in favour as an animal suitable for drawing carts in urban areas.

Ponies were regularly used for taking bags of hay to the moorland sheep. This farmer was out shepherding, with a raincoat and doubtless a few sandwiches to sustain him during his hours away from home.

In the Dales spring, the cock lapwing tumbles in the air with a reedy call and then alights to stand, bright-eyed, with long and shining head crest, on the upland pastures. The species is known in the Dales as the "tewit" and any tussocky wet area is referred to as "tewit grund". Before great tracts of land were improved by draining and ploughing, with governmental grants, the lapwing was very common — useful, too, because it consumed insects harmful to farming.

I recall a railwayman's wife at Aisgill telling me that one year, as she hung out her washing on the rough land beside her railway cottage, she had to be careful not to stand on a tewit's nest. Farmers and their men often brought back to the house a capful of eggs to make a meal. The law now frowns on this practice.

Go near the nest when the eggs are hard-set or the chicks have appeared, and a parent bird will produce an "buzzing" with tufty wings as it circles, calling with great anxiety. Crows and other predators are daringly harried.

An American referred to our walls as "those cute stone fences". Visitors marvel at the field boundaries made without mortar which, in many cases, have stood for a century and more. A wall becomes gapped if the land shifts or there is a particularly severe winter [gaps are apt to appear during the thaw which follows a long period of frost]. Then a wall is "singled up" until there is time to pull it down to the ground and re-built in time-honoured fashion.

A Dales wall is really two walls in one, set side by side, bound together by "throughs", packed with small pieces of stone and provided with a substantial row of topstones [or "capstones"]. The wall tapers as it rises. Quickness of the eye and much skill is needed by the waller, who usually prides himself on not picking up the same stone twice. One waller remarked: "Every cobble has its face, but it isn't any fool can find it!"

The Swaledale sheep is the premier breed. The type was set by farmers living on and around Tan Hill. It has swept westwards into Lakeland and eastwards to the North York Moors.

The Craven district has its own type of sheep, known as the Dales-bred [pictured here], and this breed evolved when farmers met in Upper Wharfedale to establish the most suitable type. The Swaledale has a black face and grey muzzle. So has the Dalesbred, with the addition of a white flash on either side of the nostrils.

Dales sheep were semi-wild and ran off if anyone approached them. Now they are inclined to advance on visitors, hoping for food. Today's sheep are better fed and cared for than were earlier generations.

When I broached the topic with a North Ribblesdale farmer and mentioned the boldness of the sheep, he put a hand into the calf bucket he was carrying and drew out one of the nourishing food pellets which augment the fare of sheep before and during lambing time. "It's these things that have made the difference," he said. "I reckon you could tame lions wi' 'em!"

Tups are held back so that the hill ewes do not part with their lambs too early in the spring. Winter is slow to release its grip on the uplands. The lambing time of 1988 was exceptional, a mild winter being followed by dry and not unduly cold weather.

In wild, wet conditions, many lambs are chilled through and must be given extra nutrition by the farmer. I recall my father-in-law bringing lambs into the kitchen of his farmhouse and leaving them for a while in the oven, the door of which was left open, of course. He might also be seen to plunge a hot poker into milk to warm it up and also, presumably, ensure that any germs had been destroyed.

Out of doors, the lamb is nudged to its feet by the ewe and soon takes its first drink of rich milk. It follows mother as though tied to it by string. While walking in Ribblesdale, I noticed that one farmer — anxious that ewes should be re-united with their offspring after being moved from one area to another, had painted numbers on the fleeces of the animals.

Without his dog, the farmer would not find it possible to run sheep on the fells. There must be a speedy way of rounding them up again for one of the seasonal operations like clipping or in advance of a blizzard. Some people make clear distinctions between the collie of the sheepdog trials field and the collie of the hill farm. The working dog sometimes barks to rouse laggard sheep from the bracken. Barking would be a serious fault on the trials ground.

I chatted with a Swaledale farmer who had just sent his old dog up a nearby hillside to bring in the cows for milking. "It's a little lame — like me," he explained. I suggested that the cows would know his whistled commands as well as the dog. The farmer smiled and remarked: "They know the sound of my motor-bike even better!" And he set off on two wheels — without the dog.

Agricultural shows, an important feature of the summer months, have developed greatly in recent years. When our photograph was taken in a quiet corner of the showground at Malham, a Dales show was a local event. Some shows have achieved great popularity, over 12,000 people having been recorded at Kilnsey, in Wharfedale.

At the first shows, over a century ago, the interchange of ideas among farmers and landowners gathered in a single field led to quite rapid agricultural developments. Magazines about practical aspects of farming were uncommon then. The continuing high quality of Dales livestock derives much from the friendly rivalry on the showground.

Those who attend shows today expect to be entertained by such as horse-racing, trotting or even motor-cycle racing. A recent Malhamdale Show was attended by a drove of cattle brought by a television company and featuring in a film they were "shooting" about the droving days.

The Dales summer is generally cool and cloudy. Farmers used to wait for a "window" in the weather, when they might make hay. In the picture are members of the Middleton family of Deepdale, deftly using rakes to spread the hay and expose it to the sun's rays and any drying breeze. It was not uncommon to see a minor whirlwind, drawing up wisps of hay and signifying a coming break in the weather.

Haytime was hard but satisfying work, disturbed from time to time when womenfolk arrived with cans of tea and baskets of home-baked food. One Wensleydale farmer insisted on having a hot meal served in the meadow, and his wife complied with his wish.

Another year, haytime was "chancy", with not enough breaks in the weather to allow for drying and transportation. There developed a wearying routine of putting the hay into small heaps known as "cocks", which would be broken out and re-made several times before the dryness of the hay satisfied the farmer.

Today, machines trundle across the meadows, cutting and harvesting the grass green, as silage.

This large meadow near Barden Tower, in Wharfedale, is being worked during a difficult summer. Half the field is in footcocks and the man on the tractor turns swathes. The coming of machines speeded up the operation.

When the photograph was taken, the baling machine was absent. The hay was carted from field to barn and forked from the cart through a "forking hole" on to the mew [mewstead]. In due course, the mew had to be cut into with a large knife before hay could be served to the cattle. Spores from hay that was not sufficiently dry gave many a farmer a lung infection.

The tractor is a "lile grey Fergie" [Ferguson], which Dales farmers found was a near perfect successor to their old pony. The tractor could reach awkward places and was low-geared and thus safer than most on steep fellsides. Some "grey Fergies" are still being used on remote farms.

YOUNG LOOK-ALIKES AT A DALES SHOW

KEEN SPECTATORS AT A SHEEPDOG TRIAL IN THE DALES. ONE COLLIE IS
BEING RESTRAINED BY A CROOK SLIPPED THROUGH ITS COLLAR!

Summertime Encounters. Top, left — A shepherd among the "rush-bobs" on the gathering grounds of the big dalehead reservoirs that were made by Bradford Corporation in Nidderdale. Above — The characterful face of a man of Gouthwaite, an area of upper Nidderdale where flooding took place to provide a head of water to compensate riparian owners. Left — Young and not-so-young in earnest conversation at a Dales show. They carry their best setting-off crooks!

Thwaite, under Kisdon, was named by the Norsefolk after a clearing in the native woodland. Some impressive trees remain, to delight us in their full summer foliage; the dark greens are complimented by the light greens of the old-fashioned hay meadows.

Norse words form the language of local topography — beck and scar, tarn and gill among them: short, sharp words for a people who, like many modern dalesfolk, do not waste a lot of time on verbal frills.

Visitors call at the Kearton Guest House for a meal, selecting the main course and finding tarts on the table for their later delight. Those visitors who stroll between the houses find many interesting architectural features, including a carved lintel. The pictures are of birds and beasts and the inscriptions down the side refer to Richard and Cherry Kearton, born in 1862 and 1871 respectively. The sons of a gamekeeper, they were born in this very house at Keld. Eventually, in London, they became renowned as pioneers of wildlife photography and early popularisers of natural history.

Our photograph of Thwaite was taken from where the Buttertubs Pass from Wensleydale reaches the road in Swaledale.

On a hill farm in the Dales, the new year opens in November, when the tups are "loosed". As the year dies grandly with a flurry of autumn-tinted leaves, new life is implanted in the yows. The Swaledale tup sales held at places like Hawes and Kirkby Stephen are well patronised by farmers who wish to introduce a "change of blood" into their flocks. Our photograph is of the Campbells of Horton-in-Ribblesdale in the days when Dales-bred sheep were of great significance in the limestone country.

Thousands of pounds are paid for the best tups.

At the approach of mating time, animals may be chained together, horn to horn, to stop them fighting. Two aggressive animals face each other at a distance and charge, the thwack of the impact sometimes being heard in the next parish. If any animal knows the miseries of headache it is a Swaledale or Dales-bred tup that has been fighting!

The farmer keeps up-to-date with the nuptials by spreading a strong dye on the underparts of the tups. He thus knows which yows have been mounted.

In this 1930s photograph, Mabel Sharpe, who for many years presided over White Scar Cave in Chapel-le-Dale, looks from the limestone of the Scar to where Ingleborough rises, powdered white with snow. Mabel, seen in silhouette, has with her some potholing gear. She was a keen potholer and climber in the inter-war years.

The Cave Rescue Organisation, now 50 years old, has rescued many from the underground system that honeycombs the limestone of North Craven. It is the largest outcrop of limestone in Britain.

In spring and summer, a walk on the limestone scars, stepping from clint to clint, is given added interest by the profusion of plants in the grykes, the deep crevices where the remnants of the old woodland flora survive, sheltered from the wind — and the restless teeth of the local sheep.

George Truelove, of Austwick, was the archetypal village shop-keeper, skilled in the ways of ordering, conserving and selling products which then were bought in bulk and now come in packets or tins. The outside of his establishment was encrusted with metal advertisements for products never heard of today. An outbuilding contained an ancient Austin car with which he taxied people to Clapham station or Settle when asked.

George's shop was flavoured with a hundred scents that combined into a not unpleasant odour. He coped without a refrigerator. He was perpetually weighing out commodities, including sweets, which were then poured into a cone of paper his nimble fingers had created from a single sheet, with a twist at the bottom of the cone to ensure stability.

The village shop-keeper managed to survive — just — until the coming of the urban supermarkets presented too great a challenge to a people who had the high mobility provided by the motor car. The shops that remain today are often in remoter villages, reckoning to do best when larger shops are closed or by catering for the holidaymaker. Some have an assured income because the shopkeeper is also the sub-postmaster.

LIFE IN THE VILLAGE

THE BISHOP OF BRADFORD, in his monthly Letter to the Diocese for March, 1988, referred to a new Commission on Rural Areas. "The village can no longer be taken for granted," he wrote. "Far-reaching changes are taking place in the countryside. The romantic ideal of the 18th century, with rural communities seen as self-contained places of work and residence, where familial and occupational roles interweave, no longer applies."

He assessed the situation for the Church as both complex and demanding. "New technology and increased efficiency have produced a sharp decline in employment on the land with consequent job migration. A domino effect has resulted in a loss of low-cost housing, shops and services like transport, educational and medical facilities . . . The village is no longer a cohesive social group with a common identity. It has become a community of choice, a community of communities, often of competing groups with contrasting and sometimes conflicting interests."

In the 1930s, Dales villages handy for town or city were being urbanised. The opening of a railway to Threshfield in 1901 brought changes to Grassington. The railway was closed but the impetus for development has caused the village to grow in size and importance until it now has the appearance and status of a small town. I chuckle at the sight of Bridge End, the terrace of red-tiled houses which, at the time it was built, appealed to the Bradford businessman who could commute by train. Bridge End was called Boiled Egg Row because of the time taken for the businessman to walk from station to his home!

Grassington when I first knew it in the 1930s was a shabby place, with a farmyard tang. The Grassington of today is smart, with a variety of elegant tourist shops as well as the usual run of businesses. At Grassington, the transformation came about through a healthy discontent. About 1960, most local people were admitting that the place had become shabby. Local pride suffered when the cobblestones in the main street were covered with tarmacadam. The Square was an eyesore, with uneven cobbles, unwholesome toilets and an array of telegraph poles. The Chamber of Trade organised events that raised £3,000 for re-cobbling the Square, the work being carried out in 1972.

Grassington re-asserted itself as a community when it seemed that it might become little more than a satellite to Skipton. Housing development on both the Grassington and Threshfield sides of the Wharfe has created a large community with a vibrant social life. Annual events include a major art exhibition in summer and a Dickensian festival at Christmas.

Further up the Dales, beyond Commuter range, the spare properties have been taken up as "week-end cottages" or retirement homes. Askrigg in Wensleydale has kept its typical Dales appearance, being a group of buildings of native stone and slate, with a background of pasture and moorland. The story of Askrigg has been well-told by Marie Hartley and Joan Ingilby, who live at the edge of the village. Most visitors photograph Cringley House, opposite the church, because the exterior was selected to represent the vet's home in the popular James Herriot television films, based on the author's books about life in the Dales in the 1930s. Askrigg has

HUBBERHOLME CHURCH, BY THE HEADWATERS OF THE RIVER WHARFE.

been re-vitalised and Cringley House is one of the properties of the Askrigg Foundation, which was established as charitable trust in 1971, the initiative being taken by the Rev. Malcolm Stonestreet. The Foundation also operates an outdoor pursuits centre at Low Mill.

Thwaite, when viewed from the Swaledale end of the Buttertubs Pass, is typical of a dale head village and seems uniformly old. The buildings cluster together, as though for mutual comfort, with Kisdon Hall rising beyond. Such a village has an unpretentious architecture and, happily, few signs of modern work. A carved lintel at one of the greystone cottages at Thwaite features Dales birds and beasts and marks the birthplace of Richard and Cherry Kearton, who were pioneers of wildlife photography and among the first great popularisers of natural history. Down at Muker, their names are on plaques outside the former school; it was here that they received their education. Muker names the local watercourse — it is not the river Swale, as many suppose — and camping and caravanning form a summertime spectacle, the tents being like multi-coloured mushrooms in the pastures. Such activity brings income to updale families without leaving a permanent mark on the dale.

Arncliffe and West Burton have changed little over the years. Each has a village green, so most of the houses are on nodding terms with each other. Arncliffe, the only settlement on the south bank of the Skirfare, is in a landscape of limestone scars and the church is dedicated to a fine old north-country saint, Oswald. West Burton, lying just off Wensleydale, has an in-between situation, being handy for Walden and Bishopdale.

Traditions die hard in the villages of the Dales. Austwick holds its herd-letting in February; details of discussions are entered in a calf-bound minute book first used in 1814. No longer do shepherds offer their services. The farmers chat about mutual problems like walls and the stocking of the big upland pastures. Bainbridge hears the forest horn nightly in winter; at other times the horn reposes in the main passage of the *Rose and Crown*. Tiny Hubberholme, near the source of the Wharfe, has its "land letting", with the vicar and his wardens conducting the proceedings in the *George*. This inn lies just across the river from a church which, in its obscurity from the centre of Diocesan affairs, retained a rood loft when others had to be destroyed with the demise of the Old Faith. Also in the grey building is a modern organ. The technology behind this was described to me as "an off-spin of the American space programme"!

Two contrasting villages are Greenhow, strung across the hilltop between Grassington and Pateley Bridge, and Reeth, in a conspicuous position where the upper valley of the Swale begins to broaden and become softer in tone. Each village has its tourist appeal, Greenhow being noted for its caves and Reeth through the excellence of its folk museum — also its profusion of shops and cafes. Greenhow is strung along the road at a height reaching 1,200 feet. Reeth is set around capacious greens, with views all around of the heathered "tops".

In the upper Dales, a town like Hawes is of a size which elsewhere would give it a village status. It is the capital of the upper dale, the point of convergence for families living over a wide area. Each Tuesday there is a movement of people over t'Buttertubs from Upper Swaledale, the families finding that Hawes is much more handily placed for them than is Richmond. Hawes is a staging post for visitors. Hemmed in by the Pennines, its people tend to look to the east, the native speech being more closely related to the eastern region than to that of the west. A Dent man bore this out, instancing the Dent word for being chilled — *carled* ("thou can spell it how thou likes") whereas in Hawes it is *cawld*. Northallerton — "it's knocking up 40 miles away" — has the hospital to which the seriously ill of Hawes district are taken. The bus service originates at Darlington. "We tend to play pop about t'bus service, and then realise we should be supporting it better. Most folk now seem to have a car." Hawes shopkeepers do not seem to be

KEASDEN METHODIST CHAPEL, IN NORTH CRAVEN, WAS PACKED WITH WORSHIPPERS WELL WITHIN LIVING MEMORY AND IS NOW CLOSED.

commercial rivals at all; they actually help each other out! A visitor had noticed a "lot of to-ing and fro-ing . . . I called at one shop. When the owner hadn't got what I wanted, he slipped out and got it for me — at a shop lower down the street!"

A village is in a process of constant change. The small stone settlement which looks half as old as time has, if you wander around it, some modern embellishments. In southern parts — in Commuterland — the old village has become little more than the venerable core of a settlement consisting largely of bungalows. The rural culture has been swamped by urban ideas.

Profound changes have occurred in the social and business life of the villages. When village folk lacked high mobility and did not wander far from home, the chapel, in particular, was also a social centre. In the 1930s, village halls were being built or some old wooden huts from the 1914–18 war were having their active lives prolonged by skilful "fettling". It was said of one hut that during a dance the whole structure moved perceptively in the Lancers.

Most villages had their craftsmen — blacksmith, joiner, tinsmith. Soon these came into competition with the urban-based businesses which, with improved transport and roads, were able to offer speedy services. Money which once circulated in a rural area began to stream out of it to the towns.

A Dales chapel with an isolated position, serves a scattered farming community. The worshippers converge from places up to five miles away. Mount Zion, at the head of Garsdale, stands near one of the big bridges of the Settle–Carlisle railway. It is said that navvies helped to build the place of worship. Railway and Chapel grew up together, and each was fully operational in 1876. Usually referred to as Hawes Junction, the Chapel is unpretentious and consists literally of one room, with a steeply-pitched roof and a porch stuck on the front, almost as though it were an afterthought.

The main walls must be made of elastic, for on one recent Good Friday over 100 people were accommodated, joining in the lusty hymn-singing, listening to an equally lusty "message" and then tucking in to supper. "I've never seen such a spread," said one of the visitors. "It's like a wedding feast." Each person could eat as much as he or she wished — for 60p. A supper on the same generous scale is provided at the time of the Chapel Anniversary. One July, the Sedbergh Circuit took part in a family service. The Chapel was so crowded that some people spent the whole afternoon out of doors.

When I visited the Chapel in 1984, Mrs. Jenny Thornborrow, who had been associated with it since 1943, was organist, Sunday School teacher, treasurer, caretaker and steward, as well as being a local preacher — a state of affairs not uncommon at the smallest of the Methodist chapels where a once-large congregation has shrunk, for a variety of reasons, to just a few folk and children.

Some years have gone by since the Chapel held a Love Feast, a service of testimony during which water and biscuits were passed round. Local people still talk about the Camp Meeting and Love Feast at which there were 70 testimonies. Junction Chapel is rarely crowded today, but the building endures. It was built in the era of railway expansion and, the Methodist minister observed: "Lack of money, linked with a conviction to build, has produced a simple, honest building which can hold its head up against some of the more florid structures of the period."

Dozens of rural chapels have been closed. I know of only one instance of Methodist services being held in a farmhouse, which in the early days was a common occurrence, the survival being at Mill Dam, near Bentham. The last time I conducted a service there, a rostrum was slipped over the back of a chair in the sitting room, the congregation sat on forms and I lifted up mine eyes unto the hills, for through the window was an impressive view of Ingleborough. Parish

The dancers in the photograph were performing near the cross at Giggleswick. For many, the 1930s were the lean years, a period of industrial depression. Yet in that uncertain decade, a host of people "discovered" the countryside. An earlier upsurge of interest in things English had led Vaughan Williams to collect the strains of ancient folk songs. Cecil Sharp had become nationally renowned for his research into folk dancing.

In the Dales, Miss L.M. Douglas of Giggleswick inculcated an interest in folk dancing, raising one, then two teams in the Settle area, and organising annual tours of the Craven Dales. She also found time to chat with old folk so that she might record the melodies and dance steps from the village "hops" of long years ago.

Miss Douglas published two collections: the first, "Six Dances of the Yorkshire Dales", which appeared in November, 1931, ran to 13 editions. The second book, titled "Three More Dances of the Yorkshire Dales", also featured a traditional long sword dance.

She was amazed at the enthusiasm of quite old people when demonstrating the steps of old dances. Of an event at Rathmell, she wrote: "Nothing seemed to tire them. We finished up with a polka. Tom Robinson quite danced his partner off her feet. Mrs. Frankland of Little Bank, Tom Robinson and Phineas Harrison showed us some Yorkshire step-dancing . . ."

churches have survived, but through re-organisation a clergyman finds himself in charge of several churches over a wide area. Many of the rambling vicarages have been sold.

In Ribblesdale, a friend recently lamented: "We've lost the village school, which is sad. The village shop has gone. We've still got the church, but there's no resident vicar . . ." The school had been used for dances. "A dance was a tremendous social event, particularly after the first war. There'd be people sitting on the forms round the room; people sitting on their knees — and people sitting on *their* knees, if it was a 'good do', while the rest danced in the middle. Now a lad wants to go in a car with a girl to Skipton or some other town where there's a night club with some drink and supper. It's sad, really."

In the 1930s, when folk dancing was popular, Miss L.M. Douglas of Giggleswick toured the Dales to gather information about traditional dances. Old men demonstrated the steps and hummed the tunes. She recorded the Yorkshire Dales dances, music and instructions, in two booklets that were extremely popular and now are scarce. Most Dales families were once aware of Square Eight, Huntsman's Chorus and Brass Nuts; of Kendal Ghyll, Turn Off Six and Meeting Six — all danced to music provided by fiddle or melodion. The tradition of recording dances continues. Harry Cockerill, of Askrigg, showed me a booklet produced by the Folk Dance and Song Society in 1973. One item related to *Varso Vianna,* details of which had been collected from a member of the Beresford family and from Harry. The dance was said to be of Scandinavian origin, being "not very popular, but done occasionally." Two Dales versions are acknowledged, and minor arguments break out as to which is the original style. The oldest is probably that associated with Stalling Busk, the hamlet overlooking Semerwater, where *Varso Vianna* is performed fairly slowly, even sedately. Elsewhere in the dale, it has been performed at "a gallop". Harry is in no doubt which should be used. He was taught *Varso Vianna* by Mrs. Simpson of Stalling Busk, a pianist with quite definite ideas as to the speed. It was the slower version. This is Harry's style and, as he told me, "it doesn't get folk out o' breath." Peter Beresford, who keeps alive the family tradition of playing for old-time dancing, introduced *Varso Vianna* to Austwick and other places in the far west.

Dales dances were held wherever there was room and a dancer could not become "leg-locked". At Muker, in Swaledale, dances took place in an upper room near *The Farmer's Arms,* the room being flavoured by the smell of horses that were stabled beneath. In a barn at Douk Ghyll (Craven), a cart cover was stretched across the barn doors to cut down the draught. On that occasion, Harry Wilson's Band, from Settle, wore topcoats and mittens throughout and were paid 10s for playing from 8 p.m. until 4 a.m., with an interval for supper. Kit Graham's Band, also from North Craven, used a handcart to transport a piano to the villages. At Hawes, two rival clubs — Liberal and Conservative — vied with each other and an annual ball included a knife and fork supper.

In a long career as an accordion player, Harry Cockerill imparted a Dales flavour to each dance. My wife and I often danced to music provided by Harry's little band, but not until 1982 did I have a chat with him about his musical life. He confessed that he did not know a note of music and that "my type of dance music is just the same as it's ever been. I can't play any different." A pause. "I've played the same tunes since I started — and they still dance to 'em!"

Harry Cockerill perfected his technique with the piano accordion when he lived alone for six years at High Greenfield Farm, on the gathering grounds of the river Wharfe. During that period, which was prior to his marriage, he was one-and-a-half miles from the next habitation and therefore no one heard any "wrong notes". Harry, diffident, even shy, went to dances for the sheer joy of playing. His long association with Stalling Busk began in the 1930s. On some

PARISH PUMP TALK AT LONG PRESTON. THE PUMP IS OUTSIDE THE ROW OF ALMSHOUSES, WHERE THE VICAR IS SEEN TALKING TO A PARISHIONER. THE ROW IS NOW MODERNISED AND OCCUPIED BY PEOPLE OF ALL AGES.

Royal occasion, every band — "even those that were not so good" — got a booking. And that, Harry told me, was where he came in . . . He travelled from his remote farm on a motor cycle, using cow bands to fasten the accordion case, to the machine. He chuckled at the remembrance of an old Army hut in Coverdale. The hut had a sloping floor, with the stove at the lowest point. Dancers who had drunk too much worked hard to keep away from the stove!

John Oswald Dinsdale, of Hawes, told me of jobs that were "blood for money" — the shoeing of stags [young horses] brought direct from the fells for sale at Hawes to those who needed a spirited animal for shaft work in towns. John reckoned that by the time he had finished shoeing it, the animal was half broken-in. A dodge was to strap an old pair of trousers padded with straw to the back of a horse or pony to get it accustomed to being ridden!

One of the nastiest jobs a blacksmith was called upon to do was knocking "wolf" teeth from the mouth of a horse; these teeth formed behind the useful grinders, hindering it from eating. A wolf tooth was removed — by hammer and chisel. The animal would not permit a second blow to be made. At Clapham, the smith had a horse-hair sofa for sufferers from toothache who arrived to have the painful teeth removed by pliars. "You could escape — up to the point where he got his knee on your chest," an old man of Keasden related.

It was at Kildwick, in 1953, that I heard from the Sibcy family of rapidly changing times. The family had taken over the smithy 10 years before and had lived through the bloodless revolution during which horse-power became mechanical h.p. George Henry Sibcy remembered a day on which 22 horses were shod; he had seen 15 standing patiently outside, awaiting attention, but the number had fallen to two or three a day.

At Bolton Abbey, Arncliffe and other smithies I was fascinated to see the doors bearing hundreds of brand marks — the trials made when the smith had been making brands for horn-burns for marking sheep. At Austwick, where I once lived, it amused me to see Jackie Holme sitting outside his smithy on a summer Sunday with, just above his head, the sign — *J. Holme: Ornamental Smith.* Jackie was a man who was a true craftsmen; you never heard him describe himself as such! It was fascinating to see the glow of the fire coaxed into life by the bellows; to hear the ringing of the hammer against metal as he deftly shaped a shoe on the anvil, and interesting, though not particularly pleasant, to inhale the acrid fumes when the red-hot shoe burnt into the foot of a horse as it was positioned before being nailed into place.

At Middleham, in Wensleydale, the farrier is still a busy man; elsewhere, the old-time blacksmith is scarce. The man who could make a good living fitting shoes to horses had eventually to diversify, many into the realm of wrought iron gates. When I last chatted with Alf Limmer, of Settle, he had just been asked to make the ironwork for a barbecue to be installed in a Wharfedale garden.

M'duke Miller, of Arncliffe, used to tell of the local cobbler in the 1930s who had a shop for the local trade and also cycled to adjoining villages for orders and repairs. It was a time when more and more people were buying ready-mades; repairs had to make up for the fall in sales. His boots had been excellent. "They'd turn owt till they were soled; then t'watter sometimes gits in."

BRASSES WHICH ONCE ADORNED HORSES NOW FIND A READY SALE FOR HOUSEHOLD DECORATION.

"GETTING ABOUT"

AFTER SHANKS PONY came the Dales pony. For as long as anyone can remember — and for many years before that — the farmers of the northern dales used this miniature cart horse to perform the heavy jobs. It had a variety of names, including Dales pony and Dales cob. To many farmers, this indomitable yet sweet-tempered breed was known as "t'Dales Gallowa'". This was a grand little shaft horse, with strength and stamina. It was economical to keep a Dales pony, for it thrived on waste ground where many another breed would have starved. This Dales type derived its strength and stamina from the fell pony, which was known as a "fell gallowa'". The Dales is said to have derived from the Norfolk cob its stocky build, its sprightliness and its hackney action.

Farmers, with their little sloping fields, found the broad-chested breed invaluable in the shafts of a cart or a haytime mowing machine. When used for "jagging" (taking hay to the sheep) the pony would easily carry two sacks of hay, each sack containing about a hundredweight. It was not unknown for the farmer to ride between the sacks! A pony used between the shafts of a Dales cart at muck-spreading time soon revealed its intelligence. In those days the manure was carted and then placed in heaps across a field, each heap being some seven yards from the others. A Dales pony soon developed the knack of stopping at seven-yard intervals.

The animals were harnessed to traps for trips to the weekly mart. Bill Alderson, of Swaledale, told me: "We had a grey mare. When she set off for Hawes, she hardly broke t'stroke till we got out at top o' Buttertubs. Then she would quieten down a bit, for she was frothing." In Upper Wensleydale, an early morning sight was that of a Dales gallowa' drawing a milk float to the railway station. With its ability to draw a cart holding 15 cwt, the Dales pony was a good tradesmen's horse.

The owner of a desirable stallion took his animal round the district, announcing his journey in advance so that farmers could bring their ponies to the stallion to be served. An uncastrated stallion was known as an "entire". Askrigg Hill Fair, in Wensleydale, was a noted assembly place for ponies and horses. A high percentage of them had been broken in for work. Dales ponies could be purchased at Tow Law in Durham and at Romaldkirk Fair in Teesdale. The noted fairs for horses were Appleby (just before haytime) and Brough Hill (in September).

Annie Mason, of Hawes, told me that as a young woman just after the 1914–18 war, she frequently drove a horse and trap from Burtersett to Garsdale (t'junction) to deliver her father, James Pratt, to the station in time to catch an early train to Scotland. Once she went in a nightdress with a coat thrown over it. They had been late astir, followed by a rush to catch the train. As she drove the horse and trap back through Appersett, an old lady came out of a cottage and offered her a warming cup of tea.

A few old people remember busy days at Bolton Abbey railway station, when horse-drawn wagonettes waited for the trains, ready to take day-trippers on a tour of the district. The Midland Railway was urged by one writer to avoid bringing too many visitors because of "the tendency of

SETTLE–CARLISLE TRACTION. ABOVE – RIBBLEHEAD VIADUCT (Peter Fox). BELOW – GARSDALE (from a painting by Alan Fearnley).

trippers to take rare flowers away and leave a lot of litter." One Bank Holiday, 10 coaches hired by Thomas Cook arrived late because of the rail congestion at Skipton.

Lord Peel, of Gunnerside Lodge, in Swaledale, mentioned to me the influence of the railway in opening up the grouse-shooting. Then cars provided the sportsmen with high mobility. Even so, journeys to the Dales were not undertaken lightly. "In my father's day at Gunnerside — the early 1950s — I remember seeing wonderful cars, including Daimlers and Rolls Royces, arriving up here in August. It was considered quite an achievement to have driven up from Suffolk or from London. One man mentioned that he had done it without an effective handbrake or footbrake; he had driven entirely on the gears!" Lord Peel's father described the 40 mile journey from the family home in Lancashire to the shooting lodge at Gunnerside as The Great Trek!

I asked a man in Upper Swaledale about the state of the roads in the 1930s. He replied: "They used to get stone out of local quarries and roll it in." Jack Longster, of Pateley Bridge, recalled when the road up the Banks to Greenhow Hill was waterbound, "all limestone dust." High quality cars, including Bentleys and Bugati's, raced up the Banks in competition. The 1930s were lean years in the upper Dales. Cars were uncommon. "They were mostly motor-bikes," I was told by Laurie Rukin of Keld.

Dent station, at a height of 1,100 feet above sea level, stands on the famous Coal Road that originally served a number of bell pits and extended across the tops to Garsdale. From the station, the road descends, steep and winding, into the dale. Happily for the horses that were employed transporting goods, the heavy loads were borne downwards and the carts were usually drawn up empty. Rowley Sanderson created a sensation in 1936 when he became the first man to visit Dent station with a motor lorry. He collected hay for delivery to John Oversby, of Coat Faw. Another much-needed commodity was paraffin, which was transported in barrels. Goods trade was important to Dent station, for in 1935 the income from the sale of passenger tickets was only £35 a month.

Within living memory, the butchers who came round Malhamdale with the joints of meat had a horse-drawn trap or a flat cart with a box on the back. "I remember Frank Hardisty at Gargrave buying his first car for £3. It was one of those with a 'dicky' seat in the back. He dispensed with that seat and got a joiner to fit a box. He started coming round the villages and farms with that car, selling meat."

The country garage had become established in the 1920s, the garageman taking over many of the tasks that had previously been carried out by the blacksmith. By the early 1930s, one Dales garageman had 13 second-hand motor cycles for sale. He could not persuade anyone to invest in this economic form of transport.

Fred Ellis was a pioneer garageman at Settle, and Walter Morrison, who was called "the Craven millionaire", the district's best-known resident. When he decided to buy a Fiat, his 75-year-old coachman drove the horse transport into town and was given a crash course on the car, which he had then to drive up the steep brow to Malham Moor! Morrison hired a Wolseley car from mine-host of the "Golden Lion". He would have it for a week or two and be conveyed to the Lakes. Fred used to recall: "All he did was go up and come back in it — he didn't need it during the holiday itself. And he was taciturn. When the car was driven into the forecourt of our garage at Settle, we'd see Walter almost filling the back seat, his face buried in his newspaper. He wouldn't know if he'd stopped or not!"

The story of how the first Model T Ford reached Cam Houses, at the head-waters of the Wharfe, was told to me by Kit Calvert. Bob o' Cams, a member of the Lambert family, was fond of ale. He often visited Hawes, and drinking was part of the attraction. When the Model T Ford

Right – Shank's Pony. Post-man in upper Swaledale. He was walking towards Raven Seat. Below – An early motor vehicle at Clapham. In the background is the old Manor House. Bottom – Horse work in upper Tees-dale. The horse is pulling a hay-sweep.

WHEN THE DALES BUS HAD A CONDUCTOR. MEETING OF TWO CREWS ON SERVICE 127. CONNECTING RIPON AND HAWES, IN WENSLEYDALE.

first appeared in the Dales, Bob met an agent and concluded that if he showed interest in a "Tin Lizzie" he might be treated to a pint of beer. To the delight of the agent, Bob said that he would take delivery of a car but would pay for it only when it arrived at the door of the farm. The pint of ale was forthcoming, but the car was never delivered. The agent did his best. He drove the vehicle through Gayle and up the long drag to Fleet Moss. The car jibbed at the three-and-a-half miles of rough track, a cul-de-sac, ending its journey at a point a mile above the lonely settlement of Cam Houses. The agent, admitting defeat, drove the car slowly back to Hawes.

The bus services of the Dales began with horse-drawn buses, such as those operated by the Chapman family in Upper Wharfedale and the Aldersons of Gunnerside. In Swaledale, Dick Guy started the first bus service in 1920, using an old Seabrook lorry, a flat-bodied vehicle on which rows of seats were fitted. The seats came from a four-in-hand horse bus and there was space for 25 passengers, who sat in the open and had a bumpy ride. The bus had solid tyres. It ran on one day of the week — Richmond market day — for two years, whereupon Mr. Guy purchased a Ford open charabanc, which took about 14 passengers. The service was discontinued in 1926 when restrictions were placed on this type of vehicle. The buses of Tim Scatchard and Percival Brothers competed on the dusty roads of Swaledale, racing each other to command patronage, to the embarrassment of local people. Eventually, Mr. Scatchard withdrew from the route and Percival Brothers commanded the trade for many years.

In the 1930s, Mrs. M.M. Lamb began to operate a bus service from the Talbot Yard at Settle to Horton-in-Ribblesdale. The 14-seater bus ended its career at Intake Brow, at Helwith Bridge, when the vehicle left the road. The blue-sided buses were later operated by E. & J.C. Alderson. Some of the best stories of early bus services in the Dales relate to "Pennine". When the service began from Skipton in the late 1920s, there was no timetable, and the departure of the first bus was so arranged that it would be convenient for a schoolteacher who lived in Gargrave and who wished to go to Coniston Cold. The first vehicle, of an American type, had 14 wooden seats covered with oilcloth. "Pennine" was founded by two brothers, Arthur and Vic Simpson, the former chosing the orange colour during a visit to Leyland Motors in Lancashire. It had been applied to a coach used by the firm's football team. Jim Windle, the first driver, thought up the name "Pennine". It was a robust title and related to the country in which the new bus company would operate.

"Pennine" soon absorbed a Gargrave service being run by Arthur Hull and the Malham run of the Parker Brothers, of Airton. They also took in the bus service which John Lamb had begun between Settle and Ingleton. "Pennine" stopped at almost every door, and in the early days a midnight bus ran from Settle to Skipton on Saturdays. Harry Fletcher, who began work as a driver in 1926, told me he gave tickets for return journeys only. "You never had time to bother with singles. Folk paid. You just shoved the money into t'bag. When one bus was being scrapped, a partition near t'driver's seat was ripped out — and behind it were dozens of coins that had slipped down when t'driver had been busy."

No official bus stops existed. When it was market day at Settle, farm women clambered aboard with butter baskets and a farmer brought to the bus a calf swaddled in sacking. Sheep were tethered to a back seat for the short journey into town. The driver of a bus collected prescriptions at Dr. Lovegrove's surgery in Settle, then went on to Shepherd and Walker to have them made up. Fish and chips were ordered by villagers who met the 9 p.m. bus out of Skipton. The driver would collect the delicacies from John Andrew's shop in the Shambles at Settle for distribution, still quite hot, on the return journey. Harry Fletcher remembered the eager throngs of passengers at each principal stop.

A PORCHED BUILDING ON THE OLD COACH ROUTE BETWEEN CLAPHAM AND INGLETON. WINDOWS IN THE PORCH GAVE A CLEAR VIEW UP AND DOWN THE ROAD.

Left – A "United" bus inspector photographed on Service 127 (Ripon–Hawes). The work of an inspector in the Dales consisted of much more than checking on the issue of tickets. It is related that one "West Yorkshire" official had to inquire into extensive damage to the bus, which had been charged by a footloose bull. One sunny day, a bus crew waiting for the time to depart from a quiet village, fell asleep — and were half an hour late!

Right – Gone are the cheerful "clippies" we used to know. Our picture was taken at the old bus depot in Grassington. In the golden age of bus travel, when vehicles were full, the woman conductor showed amazing fortitude. In a rural area like the Dales, a passenger might board a bus with a basket of eggs, some round-pounds of cheese — or even a goat!

One Saturday night, a policeman boarded the bus at Long Preston. Harry told him the bus was full — which, indeed, it was, having well over 40 people competing for the 14 seats — but the policeman pushed his way on to the vehicle. When the bus reached the next stop, some of the men who had been travelling on the running board, in the dark, came round to pay their fares. The policeman asked: "Where on earth have they been riding?" Said the quick-witted Harry: "They haven't been riding; they've been running at t'back!" Harold Dryden, who began to work for "Pennine" in 1928, had known a 27-seater "Lioness" to be so crowded that the conductor had to sit on the mudguard.

"Pennine" invested in a "Regal" in 1930. The speed limit had been raised from 20 to 30 miles an hour and private excursions were now possible to dances. When Harry Fletcher drove a day trip to Rhyll, it was considered to be very daring. He drove another party to Gretna Green, returning through the Lake District. "The passengers had never been so far before." My favourite driver, Walter Bates, well maintained the company tradition for friendliness and service. When he was brought to a halt in a snow drift near Long Preston, he kept the bus engine running well into the night and, there being no passengers, he decided to walk home along the railway. Walter was found, weary, hungry and chilled, as he struggled down the embankment close to Settle. It was not long before he was back on duty.

I sampled Service 127 of "United" — the Ripon–Hawes bus, which originally connected Harrogate and Ingleton. It is related that when one of the early buses ran out of petrol on the moorland road, the driver had to walk seven miles back to Hawes for a supply. "United" took over the service in 1930. In those days, J-type buses were used. They had pneumatic tyres, two doors — both on the nearside — and a long rope by which the bell was rung. One of the essential items of equipment was a wooden block, to be used as a chock on the steeper hills. At Howgate Bank, Askrigg, the passengers had to walk and the bus was chocked yard by yard as it roared slowly uphill. On Market days, passengers arrived with poultry hampers, eggs and rabbits.

Upper Wharfedale's early bus service was operated by the Chapman family and the vehicles were at first drawn by horses. "Kit" Chapman handled the Royal Mail and light goods as well as passengers. He was "bought out" by "West Yorkshire", yet from 1930 until 1935 a postbox was clipped to the front of the 6-25 p.m. bus from Grassington, maintaining the old link with the Post Office. The passengers did not expect to pay for any baggage they brought with them and a veteran conductor recalled for me that it was common for a farmer to hand him a brace of rabbits and a pound of cheese or butter "for thi trouble."

Private motoring was slow to develop. If a Dales farmer speculated on a car, it was usually a second-hand model. Some men taught themselves how to drive using one of the Land Cars — old Austins mainly — that were being produced by enterprising garagemen for use in the hayfield. I heard of a Land Car that had a kit of water standing on the front. The water was used to top up the radiator because "it got so hot."

Rufus Carr, of Rimington, specialised in making Land Cars. The mowing machine he attached was a quite ordinary farm mowing machine, of the sort drawn by horses, minus the shaft. It was chain-driven from the back axle of the car. "At that time there was nothing to beat it for mowing," Rufus told me. An old farmer remarked: "Eh, it'll niver mow like a couple of horses." It was tried out in a local meadow, with the farmer and one of his pals watching the operation surreptitiously from behind a hedge in the middle distance. The Austin 12 was a favourite because it was heavy, with a four cylinder petrol engine. Cars were bought at a scrapyard for as little as 17s 6d. Rufus recalled visiting the scrapyard when one of the brothers who owned it said: "We've just been reckoning up. Tha's bowt about 51 owd motors off us this

Right – Jackie Beresford, of Upper Wharfedale, whose jobs included transporting children from the remoter farms to village schools. Free transport was [and is] provided to avoid long walks in all weathers, though the grandparents of today's children recall when they set off on foot, carrying sandwiches and a piece of parkin or cake for the mid-day meal.

Left – The postman who drove a van from Hellifield to adjacent villages and farms. A Wharfedale postman who travelled on foot was fond of recalling when he reached a flooded river, which he normally forded. The farmer, standing on the other side, invited him to tie the mail to a stone and throw it across. The postman did — the postcard fell into the river and was lost. Said the farmer: "Nivver mind. Tell me what were on't."

last year."

The modification work was carried out with the help of a lad. Rufus's sister-in-law tested out each vehicle before delivery. A Land Car was supplied for £17. When he himself took a Land Car to a farm at haytime, the farmer gave it full revs and set off round the field, with an anxious Rufus running behind. "He was dead rough with it that first day; I thought that it would never last all haytime." In the event, it was used up to and throughout the 1939–45 war.

Rufus Carr also produced the equivalent of a small-farm tractor when he put two gear-boxes in an old Austin 12 car. "Farmers used them for all sorts of jobs, including muck-leading. I put a plough on the back of one of them . . ." The efficiency was increased when two tyres were used on each of the back wheels — the normal tyre and another which fitted over it. The wire rim of this additional tyre were removed and slots made to provide extra gripping.

During the 1939–45 war, tractors became a familiar sight. The "War Ag." operated Fordson tractors, which did not have tyres but rather spikes for gripping. "When a tractor was being moved from one farm to another it should have been fitted with metal bands to protect the road, but often the driver did not bother. The spikes did a lot of damage to the road surface. They said they were going to introduce some sort of fine, but they never got on with it." The Fordson was a tractor — and that was all. "There was nothing to it other than it could pull something." The Dales had to wait a little longer for power take-off shafts so that another machine could be driven by tractor power. From 1946, the little Ferguson was the work-horse on the hill farms. With a low gear, it moved safely and easily on the hills, being a worthy successor to the sure-footed Fell or Dales pony. The tractor, like the pony, had "good 'odding back power".

A few cattle wagons were on the road before the 1939–45 war, but with war in progress and with petrol rationed, journeys had to be limited. It was not unknown for the owner of a cattle wagon to ring up a farmer and arrange to meet him and his stock at some half-way point to conserve petrol. For Malham farmers who walked their stock the whole way to Hellifield, it was convenient to put them up overnight at Herries Farm, near Otterburn.

A recently introduced means of transport is now commonplace at fell farms. I refer to the motorised trike with balloon tyres that does not greatly harm the ground. One farmer's only complaint about the bike was that it was of foreign make. He owned a trike of 200cc and his brother drove one of 250cc.

A stimulating approach to Penyghent because good views of Ribblesdale can be enjoyed throughout is that which follows the green lane from Helwith Bridge. A walker does not turn his back on the dale but can glance at it, seeing the long forms of Ingleborough and Whernside and trains passing on the Settle–Carlisle line, these trains looking like toys against the majesty of the natural scene.

The route joins the Pennine Way and then ascends the hill on a path which has been greatly improved under a conservation scheme. It is permitted to sit down during the ascent and look at a dale where the landscape has been seriously blighted by quarrying but which, none the less, has much natural grandeur.

ON THE "TOPS"

THE HEATHER-DOMINATED MOORS we see today have developed over some 2,500 years following large-scale burning and destruction of upland woodlands. In high summer, the tufty heads of cotton grass, whiter than white, give the impression there has been a late snowfall on the Pennine mosses. Then, on the drier ridges, the bell heather comes into bloom. Patches of regal purple are to be seen in the moorland "mix" of coarse vegetation. Human visitors to the moors laboriously gather bilberries. The ling — our commonest species of heather — soon commands attention. On the best moors, it forms a fitted carpet of purple hue stretching from horizon to horizon. The moor, which can seem so dead in winter, is full of life in the brief, often cloudy summer. Bees fly sorties from hives set down at the moor edge; the honey they produce is dark and viscid.

Writers about the moors have stressed their bleakness. Stevenson's "vacant wine-red moor" and Charlotte Brontë's "lonely moor" are actually brimming over with life, which the researches of modern naturalists are describing in fine detail. Much has been discovered about those hardy moorland birds, the red grouse. In due course, there will be detailed studies of the upland waders — of curlew, redshank, golden plover and dunlin — which contribute to the appeal of the hills. The moorland ecology is much more delicately balanced than many of us had suspected. The plough has ripped up many an acre for re-seeding with grass and the planting of trees. Over-grazing by sheep has been more than the heather could stand and it has vanished over wide areas.

The red grouse remains faithful to its open, windswept Calluna moors. With a specialist diet, almost all of which is composed of heather, there is no option for it but to cling to the "tops". Dr. Peter Hudson, of the North of England Grouse Research Project, told me of this astonishing bird. The grouse plucks the heather with a short bill. The bird has a gut that is especially adapted for dealing with the tough and fibrous plant food. A thick plumage affords insulation against the cold and wet. Normally the plumage is rusty-brown, but a female in good condition may have a rich honey tone. The feet of the stubby grouse are feathered. The son of a Swaledale gamekeeper recalled for me the days when he was sent to the moor to "bray" the snow with a besom and expose the heather, which was food for starving grouse. Otherwise, the birds would migrate down-country and few, if any, would return.

Some of the finest grouse moors in Britain are to be found in the Yorkshire Dales, with a particularly famous tract of heather ground above Wharfedale. Many a royal personage and titled person has been at Bolton Abbey for the Glorious Twelfth — though it is never glorious for the grouse! These moors, and the vast tracts between Wensleydale and Teesdale, are at the ideal elevation for red grouse. The ritual of grouse shooting was the reason why so many updale estates were built up, providing much employment for the Dales folk. The old people remember when King George V arrived in Wharfedale for the grouse-shooting. He stayed at Bolton Hall; on Sunday, he walked to the priory church to attend the morning service. He is recalled by a

Above: Old Gang, in a Swaledale gill blighted by lead-mining. Yet grouse perch on the buildings and are relatively common round about. Left: Golden Plover, which nests where the herbage is "thin". Above – The raven. A few pairs nest and young birds from the northern Pennines over-winter in the Dales.

dalesman as "a littleish fellow with gingery whiskers; a gruff sort of man, but kind to children."

In the heyday of grouse shooting, gamekeepers burnt or "swizzened" the heather in rotation to provide a constant supply of young heather shoots, food for the grouse and sheep. "Vermin", mainly crows and raptors, were ruthlessly persecuted and the corpses displayed on a gibbet near a road, where friends and neighbours might marvel at the prowess of the keeper. At grouse shooting time, the Dales farmers provided ponies and labour for the visitors. Provisions were taken to a shooting-hut (which was usually made of stone) at the moor edge. I have visited many such huts, which invariably have two rooms and a shelter for the horse, temporarily released from the shafts. One room was for the gentry, the other for the beaters, and at one roofless building I noted that grass grew in the "better end" and nettles where the beaters crouched down to eat sandwiches and to drink tea out of flasks! Dallowgill, above Nidderdale, is a "black moor" and a hard one for sheep; it was also a tough moor for men when the Vyners of Studley presided over it. The word of the head gamekeeper was law. "If a man fell out with him," said a local farmer, "the gamekeeper would say to the landlord he thought it was time that man was going. And that man had to go!"

Grouse-shooting, says Lord Peel, is a means to an end. "You are taking the final crop. To me, the real job is management — getting involved with a unique bird." He was among those who set up the grouse research project. George Murray, the gamekeeper at Clapham, used to tell me when the drier ridges on Ingleborough were bountifully covered with heather and when the grouse were widespread. I have a photograph of the 1870s showing Ribblehead as a heather moor.

When a moor is no longer adequately keepered, the grouse come under considerable pressure from predators like crows and foxes. Yet some fine moorland estates remain. One of the best is Dallowgill, above Nidderdale, which the head gamekeeper, Tommy Guy, described to me as a "low" moor. (He was comparing it with moorland on the Northern Pennines). The ground is sandy or loamy. "We can burn in spring and the new growth has struck by summer," he said. Years ago, farmers almost fought for the privilege of cutting and transporting bracken, which they used as bedding for their stock. "Now nobody wants bracken and it's got out of hand." In the absence of farmers with scythes and a lot of patience, a helicopter is chartered to spray about 200 acres a year. In several wet summers during the 1880s, spraying was not possible.

What life was like on a large Dales sporting estate early this century was recalled for me by Major J.E.E. Yorke, of Halton Place. The Yorkes were an influential Nidderdale family for some 400 years. The estate had its own shepherd on the moor, which was "stinted", each stint representing the pasturage of a single sheep. The numbers of sheep could therefore be regulated. "The shepherd knew every sheep, so no one else's stock could infiltrate." Burning areas of heather in rotation ensured an abundance of fresh young growth but old heather was left here and there against the time of winter snow; the sheep could then nibble at the tips of heather stalks and, moving about among this young stuff, leave paths that grouse might follow. Modern moors are beset by tick, heather beetle and the insidious spread of bracken.

Bracken, once prized by farmers as bedding for the wintering stock, continues to extend its range. Peter Hudson had heard of an old custom in Nidderdale, when farmers who wanted to mow bracken lined up against a wall, and at a signal from the agent they rushed forward to claim areas of bracken. A man could remove the bracken from an area within a circle he mowed. Demarcation disputes sometimes led to blows being exchanged. Now the bracken remains unmown! The shepherd of old ensured that sheep were spread out across a moor "like a thin layer of butter". Now the sheep are left to themselves, they tend to concentrate on the lower end

Pictured here is a young curlew, as yet incapable of flight. Alerted by the parent birds, it lies low and still in a Dales meadow until the "all-clear" is sounded. The adult curlew is lanky, streaky-brown, with a long decurved bill – features which normally would not be considered attractive. Yet the curlew has a strong appeal to those who go out and about in the Dales in spring and summer.

Birds return from wintering grounds at the coast. A Wharfedale farmer says: "Thou can reckon t'back o' winter's brokken when thou hears a curlew shout!" The song-glides of a cock bird in its territory are an essential element of the Dales spring. A bird climbs steeply, then goes into a long glide during which it fills the air with a cascade of bubbling notes.

Curlews are less common than they were when fields were rougher and damp places not uncommon. Re-seeding after drainage and ploughing leads to a considerable loss of the curlew's natural food.

of the moor. Extra grazing pressure can push the heather back. Moorland fires, many of them started unintentionally by visitors, can be disastrous, for they sterilise the peat.

For his research work into the red grouse, Dr. Peter Hudson was based on Askrigg. He attached tiny radio transmitters to selected birds and, using antennae and radio-tracking equipment, he could detect the grouse at will, such as at the roosting places, where he examined the fresh droppings, revealing the bird's food on the previous day and also the disease level. Other birds in his areas for special study carried identification tabs. "The grouse need heather for food and shelter; without heather they do not exist in appreciable numbers." Heather is not a very nutritious plant, particularly in the early spring. On some moors, particularly the high wet moors of the Pennine tops, a grouse will often switch to the flowers of cotton grass because the protein content is higher than with heather at that time of the year.

Moorland birds such as the grouse, golden plover, dunlin and merlin are being eradicated by the loss of heather, partly as the result of mis-management and also through the spread of commercial forestry. Golden plover return to the moorland areas as early as February, and for a time they settle on the in-bye land to feed, the cock birds spreading to the moors to establish their territories, within which they will attract mates. The plover benefits from good management on the grouse moors, from predator control and burning in the late winter, because it nests in heathered areas where vegetation is short. The chicks need insects in the boggy areas. Dunlin nest in the high damp areas, often those with some standing water. Merlins need the heather in which to nest; they feed on meadow pipits and skylarks. Good moor management benefits each of these species. At Dallowgill, several pairs of oyster-catchers nest by the moorland becks and Canada geese have their nests in mossy places, though the goose population declined from its peak of about 150 pairs following a drainage scheme in 1980.

Not for many years until 1986 had a golden eagle been reported from the Dales. Then one appeared at Greenhow Hill and in Wharfedale. Eventually, where Hebden Gill, near Grassington, peters out in a tract of moorland, a shepherd was tending his sheep on November 21 when he found the carcase of an eagle at the foot of a pole carrying electricity cables.

Frederick Riley used to tell me of a year when there was an infestation of caterpillars, drawing in gulls from the coast. These birds, he claimed, were the founders of a small nesting colony on the tarns set high on Whernside; and here they nested for many years. Whether or not the penetration of black-headed gulls to inland nesting places began in some cases with predation on caterpillars I do not know, but this species of gull has long been established on many moorland tarns, where the eggs were harvested by local gamekeepers and farmers, especially during the wartime food scarcity. I do not care much for black-headed gulls in a moorland setting. The cries are raucous; the droppings kill off areas of heather; the stench can be strong. Even worse is a moorland colony of larger gulls, the herring and lesser black-headed species. Perhaps the most famous colony is that on the Bowland moors where at one time many acres of ground were covered by nesting birds. The few red grouse had gull droppings on their backs! I once had the stimulating experience of flying over the moors in a helicopter and looking down on a speckled moorland where the gulls nested. The colonising gulls probably came from Walney, by Morecambe Bay, where both species of big gulls became established many years ago. Gulls found rich pickings throughout the year on the tips near the big towns.

A denizen of the upland mosses is the short-eared owl, the most diurnal of our owls, which can be seen hunting by day, flying close to the ground, following each contour, hoping to catch a mouse or vole unawares. The "moss owl" benefits from the early years of afforestation with conifers. When an area has been fenced off and the trees are, as yet, too small to smother the

Nothing has changed the appearance of the Dales more profoundly than the large new conifer forest. Vast tracts of upland, formerly used for the grazing of stock, has vanished under serried ranks of sitka spruce and other trees with a reputation for rapid growth and commercial value.

A conifer forest of this type clogs the landscape after offering wildlife some good habitat for a few years. In an area like the Pennines, windblow is a problem when the trees have been growing for 20 years and more. Much planting has taken place because of the attendant tax concessions for those who put money into forestry, but changes to the law have made this less appealing and permission is unlikely to be forthcoming for any new major forest on the Pennines.

ground vegetation, these are ideal conditions for the short-tailed field vole. With an old friend, Stan Lythe, I used to watch the owls over Greenfield near the source of the Wharfe.

Upland forests change the character and appearance of some areas of the Dales, though imagination is now used in planning the forests, with various species being introduced to break up the monotony of a monoculture. An early Dales scheme of the Forestry Commission concerned a famous old sheep stray on Hope Moor, between Arkengarthdale and Barnard Castle. It is traversed by an adventurous road known as The Stang. Lines of ornamental trees were planted beside the road. Here the traditional crop of wool gave way to a new crop of wood — pit prop variety.

At Bolton Abbey, in Wharfedale, wildlife is varied and profuse in 600 acres of amenity woods at dale level, beside the river Wharfe. These woods are traversed by a popular approach to The Strid. Yet the estate includes 1,200 acres of dark, drool conifers at higher elevation. They are managed commercially under a plan approved by the Forestry Commission. In the older Deer Park, and also near Barden, are ancient oaks, many of them hollow. They must have been in their prime when the Cliffords of Skipton used the area as a hunting preserve. At Laund House is an oak estimated to be 800 years old. It looks dead but contrives to produce a few fresh leaves each spring.

My favourite "upland" area in the Pennine Dales is the head of Teesdale. The valley is noted for its white-painted farmhouses, and whenever I go that way in spring I listen for the bubbling aria of the curlew and the exhuberant "oo-ip" of the displaying cock lapwing, a bird known as a "tewit" in the Dales. The fluty aria of the cock ring ouzel sounds in the echo-chamber of a gill. A Pleistocene chill is detectable where the dale gives way to the open fells, despite profound changes caused by man, not least the creation of a reservoir to regulate the flow of the river. Crusty snow lies on these northern fells for about a third of the year. In midwinter, the temperature stays below freezing point for weeks on end, plummeting to minus 24 degrees. Yet there can be glorious, healthful days. With a high pressure system centred on Scandinavia, the sky clears, the air becomes calm and the snowfields gleam as they catch the eye of the sun.

The Upper Teesdale National Nature Reserve (8,600 acres) is the third largest in England. Much of the reserve is at an elevation of 1,600 feet. In spring, the ground is spangled by the blue flowers of the spring gentian (*Gentiana verna*), a plant confined in Britain to the Tees basin and Western Ireland. The arctic/alpine flora endures on Widdybank Fell and in neighbouring areas because of the severity of the climate and some novel soil conditions. Other floral rarities are the autumn gentian, Teesdale violet and Teesdale sandwort.

Having a tarmac road which also serves as a footpath keeps the disturbance by human visitors to the minimum. Most people keep to the path. It leads to the head of Caldron Snout, a waterfall that is like an ancient prophet crying out in the wilderness.

NOT A QUARRY BUT A NATURAL LIMESTONE FEATURE ON THE FLANKS OF PENYGHENT.

QUARRIES AND RESERVOIRS

I BEGAN this book with a description of the Yorkshire Dales as a man-made landscape. Two prominent man-made features are the quarries and reservoirs. The landscape is pock-marked by quarries, most of them quite small. Wherever old buildings are found, you can see the complimentary holes in the ground from which the stone and slate were taken. The skills of acquiring natural stone and dressing it for architectural work are almost lost, for at the time of writing not one quarry is used for that purpose. The early walls were made from material picked up when the land was cleared for farming; the more recent walls demanded large quantities of stone that had to be taken from the ground and shifted to wherever it was needed.

At Burtersett, above the Ure, the operation of removing stone for flags and buildings was really a cross between quarrying and mining. The best stone came from the drifts which penetrated the hillside for anything up to half a mile, pillars being left to support the roof. No explosives could be used and so the men used hand-drills. It was "desperate" work but relatively healthy. The quarry-workers rarely suffered from the lung troubles that afflicted the men who were employed in the lead mines. Stone was brought out by pony and truck.

On Quarry Hill, Burtersett, there were two commercial enterprises, each built up by a member of the large Metcalfe clan. The enterprises lived on fitfully until the 1920s. Stone from Burtersett, transported to Hawes railway station in two-horse wagons, was consigned mainly to the cotton towns of industrial Lancashire. Kit Calvert, who was reared at Burtersett, told me about the quarry community. Some families were large by modern standards. A cousin of Kit had 12 children, who lived in a house that had two bedrooms. In similar property, parents, four children and lodgers lived.

Where limestone obtrudes, there are small field kilns in which it could be burnt before being spread on the land. I heard that the last kiln to flare in the Settle district was on the Hunter family's land at Cowside, the fuel used being brittle coal from the Yoredale series high on Fountains Fell. Not far away, in North Ribblesdale, are huge quarries where, using modern techniques, and with a ready supply of coal available on the Settle–Carlisle railway, men like John Delaney grew rich while his men excavated and pulverised some of the purest limestone in the land.

When I moved into the Dales, I soon heard of John Delaney, of Beecroft and Threshfield quarries. Delaney even attempted to work a colliery on Threshfield Moor. His name was well-known in the days when railway wagons might be privately owned and could bear the name of the owner. His origins were in Ireland, where he was born in the "Hungry Forties", the potato crop failing year after year. The absentee landlords still wanted their rents and John's father was one of those employed to collect them. He met a violent end, being shot by smallholders, and John's eldest sister, Ann, took charge of the impoverished family. They moved to Stalybridge, in Cheshire, and it was from here that John travelled to Settle and a job in Hector Christie's mill. He became an overseer. In 1870, he was married to Annie Carver, a weaver. They were a devoted couple. In 1876, John became a Quaker.

INCLINE RAILWAY SERVING A NOW DISUSED LIMESTONE QUARRY ON MOUGHTON HILL, NORTH RIBBLESDALE.

So much for his private life. His immense drive, and the help of a Quaker banker in Sheffield, led to him leaving Christie's mill and establishing his own business, a small store at Langcliffe. He then took a brave decision to study geology at Manchester University while his wife attended to the shop. Wife and daughter Carrie worked hard but barely made enough to exist until his studies were over and he could take advantage of them by opening a limestone quarry at Horton (close to the Settle–Carlisle railway) and benefiting from the considerable demand for lime in the new industrial England.

The railway represented a relatively cheap form of transport for the coal he needed for limestone-burning; the railway was handily available to move his lime to the new industrial areas of England, and especially to Sheffield, where he had important contacts. Delaney owned private wagons, and his name became well-known. The quarry he opened at Threshfield prospered greatly. A colliery enterprise on Threshfield Moor failed. Within 15 years, and entirely through his own initiative and drive, he became an extremely wealthy man. He moved to a capacious new house at Settle but was in touch with every aspect of his business. His daughter, Carrie, "kept the books" and eventually knew as much about it as he did. Carrie was his heiress who continued to manage the Delaney enterprises after her father's death.

The Delaney story I like best is connected with the Settle–Carlisle railway, the coming of which made his Ribblesdale venture possible. Not liking Settle tap water, he arranged for a kit full of water from Horton to be transported by rail and delivered to his Settle home daily. That home backed on to the railway, and he was fond of timing the trains. In bad weather, he became uneasy if the Scots express did not pass on time, and once he roused the whole household — at 4 a.m. — because the train was excessively late. John Delaney, one of the most important of the Dales industrialists, died on Christmas Day, 1921. He willed £5 to each man in his employ at the time of his death.

I have chatted with many quarrymen. The veterans recalled when hand-drills were in use to prepare the holes in which explosives were packed. One of the most exacting jobs was performed by the breakers and fillers, who wielded great hammers and stacked up the shattered rock in tubs, wheeling them to the kilns. W. Thompson, of Horton, remembered when rough stones were picked up by hand and forks were used to gather the smaller pieces. When I met him in 1954, he had been lime-drawing for 20 years and commented that although machines had taken much of the manual work from the industry, the lime-drawers still had to sweat at their jobs.

To stand in the vast amphitheatre of Beecroft quarry was always an awesome experience; not only faith moves mountains! A few tiny trucks, the dumpers, scurried over the vast floor, their heavy wheels rousing the sleeping lime dust and sending it billowing behind as they travelled with full loads to the crushing plant, where metal jaws champed the rock into a state acceptable to the screens.

Those were the days when limestone was quarried on Moughton, above Helwith Bridge. The grey rock was brought down in tubs on an incline railway, the weight of the laden trucks carrying the empties back up the slope. A quarryman told me that Good Friday was known as "Runaway Friday". The men felt they should have the day off, but this was not allowed. So when, as invariably happened, there was a runaway and subsequent damage to the plant, they hinted to the bosses that it was a rebuke for working a day that was special to Churchfolk.

Now the quarries at Helwith Bridge concern themselves with the exploitation of Silurian flag, transported as chippings for roadwork. The stratum is vertical; the "granite" bluey-grey. It was the stuff once taken from five little quarries in this area as large slabs, to be used for flooring.

ABOVE – DAM AT COW GREEN, TEESDALE, JUST BEFORE COMPLETION. BELOW – BRADFORD'S PRIDE IN ITS
NEW RESERVOIRS IN UPPER NIDDERDALE IS INDICATED BY THIS FINELY-CARVED STONE.

benks [shelves] in farmhouse kitchens and for cisterns in which to store soft [rain] water.

Quarrying is a messy industry. Now that machines have replaced the once large labour force, the quarry face visibly recedes almost as you look at it and it is undoubtedly a considerable eyesore. The buildings are modern, utilitarian, covered with rust and dust. The day is punctuated by the thunder of explosions. If there is any consolation for those who take pleasure in the landscape, it is that a quarry no longer used has its hard features softened by wind, rain and frost, as at Craven Quarry, between Langcliffe and Stainforth. Elsewhere in the Dales, I have found spikes of orchids and nesting hawks in areas ravaged by the quarry companies and then left to recover as best they may through the natural processes.

Bradford "brass" built the reservoirs at the head of Nidderdale, in whose water is reflected the frosty gaze of Great Whernside. A spur of the Pennines was plunged waist-deep in cold water with the building of Angram (1913) and Scar House (1936). A growing city avoided a serious water shortage through the Nidd works, with their capacity to store 2,340 million gallons. Yorkshire Water Authority took over from the old Bradford Waterworks. So zealously had Bradford guarded its Nidd territories that many motorists visiting the valley thought of it as ending with a flourish of macadam in the streets of Middlesmoor. The true dalehead lay behind a gate and private notice. The Water Authority decided to admit the motoring public, within reason, by giving visitors access to the private road and making a special car park and toilet block.

The story of the Dales enterprise of the Bradford Waterworks began with a critical water situation in 1858. Plans were devised to use gathering grounds in Wharfedale and this scheme — very ambitious in itself — was later to be dwarfed by the Nidderdale works. A hundred thousand cubic yards of material were excavated to make Gouthwaite reservoir, which was completed in 1901 at a cost of £240,000. Thus did Bradford Corporation compensate the riparian owners of the Nidd for the loss of water through the dalehead reservoirs, Angram and Scar House. Walter Rayner, who was two years old when the dam was completed, told me tales of Gouthwaite Hall he heard from his grandmother, who resided there. They include details of the events — amusing in retrospect, but not funny at the time — leading up to the excavation of the building.

Mr. Barlow, of Bradford Corporation Waterworks Department, visited the family and told them that the impounded water would extend as far as their garden gate. Additional water would flow over the dam. The new reservoir did indeed reach the garden gate, lifting it from its hinges and floating it away. The engineer, revising his ideas, said the water would stop rising when it reached the doorstep of the hall; further water would flow off down the valley. Mr. Rayner's father prudently heaped sods on the doorstep to keep out the water, but it seeped between the flagstones. The carpet had to be taken up, and valued possessions were piled on a table. The flood extinguished the kitchen fire. Later that day, when objects were floating from the table, the family took to the upper floors, where they lived for a considerable time until their new farmhouse had been completed. They entered Gouthwaite Hall by means of a flight of wooden steps which were made to where a new doorway had been driven into the outer wall. The upper rooms could be used simply because the ground sloped and they could gain entry at the back!

A shallow reservoir, receiving fresh silt via the river and becks, and rich in small organisms that live in or on the mud, Gouthwaite is outstanding ornithologically. There is plenty of food for wild birds. As the daylight dwindles in winter, gulls drift in to roost on the water. Waterfowl are here in plenty. The road made by Bradford, and extending along the western shore of Gouthwaite, is a supreme viewing area for the avian visitors.

Now there is the facility to pump large quantities of water from the Wharfe into Chelker reservoir. Leeds claimed the Washburn Valley and extended its enterprise to Thruscross. Up in the north, at Cow Green, Teesdale, is a river-regulating reservoir which was intended to assuage the thirst of Teesside. Alas, much classic countryside, with its rare flowers, was desecrated at a time when, industrially, the area around the mouth of the Tees was on the downturn. The reservoir project was not as vital as we thought. The water does prettily reflect the ponderous form of Cross Fell, the highest of the Pennine peaks.

IVOR MASON AT THE OLD WENSLEYDALE PRESS, HAWES IN WENSLEYDALE.

WARTIME INTERLUDE

MANY YEARS AGO, the daughter of Harry White, who farmed Kentucky, at the head of Walden, set off from home with two horses, intending to deliver them to Arncliffe, where Harry had taken another farm. She entered Walden Moor, which forms a horseshoe of boggy ground, and the horses became "bogged". Freeing them was a major task. As it was the peak of haytime, with the weather not expected to last, dalesfolk tried to free the horses in the evening. They were not successful. The animals were painlessly destroyed. During the 1939–45 war, a German aircraft dropped a land mine on the same stretch of bog and in the explosion the bones of the long-dead horses were lifted from the ground and spread about the moor.

Sticks of bombs jettisoned by enemy aircraft returning home from raids in the far west were reported from Newby near Clapham, from Garsdale and from Malham Moor. At Newby, where a cow perished, the "krump" of high explosives startled a lady in the village. She was a wealthy woman with a home in Bristol. So severe was the bombing there, she had asked a friend to recommend an area in the country where she might sleep peacefully at night. She had just arrived at Newby when the bombs fell. At Garsdale, everyone concluded that the target was the Settle–Carlisle railway, which was not hit. On Malham Moor, local farmers stared with drooping lower jaws at some still-smoking craters near Tennant Gill Farm.

The war period brought soldiers and tanks into Skipton, the tanks ripping up roads and knocking slivers of stone from the kerbs. Catterick Camp was bulging at the seams and soldiers were sent out on manoeuvres into the Dales. For some of them it was their first acquaintance with the area. One or two were to return again and again, intoxicated by the scenery and clean air, a contrast with their urban upbringing. The Army took over the whole of the Yorkshire Wolds, and thus relaxed their hold on the Dales a little. "They went where the hell they liked on the Wolds, firing as they went." The Army tried to establish a shooting range at Grimwith, above Wharfedale, but it was not a success, the ground being too wet for tanks. "Some of the tanks just disappeared from sight in the peat and the idea was not proceeded with." A lead smelting mill at the head of Wharfedale was blown up in 1942 by soldiers who were testing a new type of explosive.

A train bearing George VI on a tour of the North stopped at Bolton Abbey, where a special air raid shelter had been constructed "in the banking". (After the war, the shelter was used by a local man as a garden shed). Bolton Abbey was used for the storage of ammunition, inviting enemy action. A bomb fell on the cricket field, another landed in the Wharfe, and a string of bombs made holes across a big field. Jim Metcalfe told me that the bombers came on a Saturday night — and that on the following day the ammunition was removed!

At the beginning of the war, urgent attention was given to the necessity of growing as much as possible on the home acres, for imported food had to be transported in convoys that were vulnerable to attacks by enemy submarines, and were wasteful in human lives as well as in the loss of valuable food and materials. In the Dales, the War Agricultural Committee arranged

ON THE SETTLE–CARLISLE RAILWAY. ABOVE – TRAPPED BY SNOW NEAR GARSDALE. BELOW – BLEA MOOR,
WHERE IN WARTIME LOOPS WERE ADDED TO THE LOCAL SYSTEM.

with local farmers a rota of ploughing on every farm. "This caused the most frightful uproar," I was told by the owner of an estate. "Dales farmers didn't like ploughing. They had no ploughs. Most of them had horses. They were told which land would be ploughed and along came a Ministry man with a tractor and a plough and tore it up. They did a lot of harm to the old drains. They were pushed for time. The result was two or three beautiful crops of oats. All but one fell down in the rain. The Dales farmer could never get a decent harvest; he could grow the stuff, but couldn't get a harvest."

A Malham farmer relates: "There were not many suitable fields for ploughing. It is quite a boney area, with not much depth of soil. We all had to plough, though my family had only to do two acres. It was not profitable, for it did not justify us buying all the equipment — a plough and a drill, a harrow and a roller, and that sort of thing. So the Ministry had to introduce the scheme of having contractors. They did everything connected with the arable schemes."

The Women's Land Army had an attractive uniform — green pullover, corduroy knee breeches, fawn knee-length stockings and brown leather shoes. A three-quarter length brown overcoat completed the outfit. At work, the WLA girl had bib and brace dungarees, black boots or gunboots and the ubiquitous wellingtons. For some, there was the excitement of driving tractors — those basic Fordsons, with spikes set in the back wheels for extra grip during ploughing. Others in the Dales had first to learn how to harness working horses. In the Craven area, hostel facilities were available for the WLA. Much of the tackle owned by the "War Ag." was kept in the capacious area behind the Town Hall, which is now the town's principal car park.

Italian and German prisoners of war appeared on our farms and even in our streets, having been let out on parole, clad in battledress with circlets of brightly-coloured material sewn on to the backs of the blouses. The prisoners were, in general, welcomed by the farmers and their families, providing much needed help. Some joined with soldiers in clearing snow from the Settle–Carlisle line during one of the grim wartime winters. A few German prisoners remained when the war was over; they had married local girls. Into the Dales, in the early days of the war, had come evacuees, many of whom had not previously seen a live cow or sheep.

Life on the farms was not seriously changed, for Dales farmers had known lean times. "Petrol rationing meant that the milk lorry no longer toured all the farms; we took our milk down to prescribed collecting points," said a Craven man, adding: "All feeding-stuffs for cattle were obtainable only through coupons. I had to fill in a form once a month to apply for coupons. Of course, there was a 'black market' in those things. Some farmers were able to obtain more coupons than they actually used. People would buy coupons at £5 apiece."

The pig came into its own. Pig-meat became part of the "black market" and stories were told of how hams and sides were shifted surreptitiously. A tale from North Ribblesdale concerns a local tradesman who was suspected by the police of black-marketeering. He always managed to evade detection until, one evening, he was returning to town in his van — a van that contained a considerable amount of pork — when he was "waved down" by a police constable. The tradesman was asked what he had in the back of the van. He replied: "A pig." The constable, fearing that he was having his leg pulled, allowed the man — and the pork — to proceed.

A system was introduced whereby a farmer presented his sheep at the auction mart and, rather than being sold by auction under a hammer, a panel of graders estimated the weight of these sheep. The farmer was paid directly by the government on the estimated weights. Notice had to be given of the stock that would be presented. There were, for a time, no auction fees — or "luck".

The Local Defence Volunteers, LDV for short and known to local wiseacres as "Look, Duck and Vanish", became the Home Guard, exchanging pitchforks for weapons and demonstrating their skills to their relatives and friends at local galas. The Home Guard was ready to protect the Dales against enemy action. One contingent was charged with caring for Ribblehead viaduct, that giant structure in blue-limestone that carries the Settle–Carlisle railway across the valley to Blea Moor. It is related that after a term of duty, the men returned to Ribblehead station, where customarily they checked the ammunition. One man insisted that he had removed cartridges from his rifle and, to illustrate the point, pulled the trigger of his rifle. There was an explosion, a whiff of acrid fumes — and a neat hole appeared in the ceiling of the station waiting room!

A cottage high on Kisdon, Upper Swaledale, was one of the many Home Guard look-outs. "I remember one neet I was up there and we heard this aero engine, which had a wavering sound. A bomb was dropped over on Stainmoor; they said he was trying to get the railway viaduct . . . A few planes came down roond about here. Tom Wilson, a gamekeeper, was head of the Home Guard and he used to organise things when a plane crashed. One time we found the pilot. He was jabbering so much we couldn't just make out what he was saying. He turned out to be one of ours!"

DETAIL FROM A STAINED GLASS WINDOW IN HUBBERHOLME CHURCH, WHARFEDALE.

The discovery of the Dales as a region worth visiting happened towards the end of the 18th century, in what became known as the Romantic Period. A curiosity about such natural wonders as Gordale Scar and Aysgarth Falls continued on an increasing scale through the 19th century, as more and more people with the money and leisure to travel were stimulated by paintings, early photographs and the first detailed guide books.

During The Great Outdoors movement of the 1930s a trickle of visitors became a torrent and now the torrent is a flood. Of guide book production there is no end; information centres dispense booklets and leaflets by the thousand, and the map-makers have been kept busy.

Modern walkers are far more conspicuous than was the walker photographed above. He was on the Three Peaks route in North Ribblesdale, some 30 years ago. Fellsides are now dotted with groups wearing waterproof clothing in a variety of brilliant shades.

AN AGE OF LEISURE

FOR MANY, the 1930s were a time of enforced leisure. They were able to explore the Dales because there was no work for them to do in their home towns and, using their feet or cycles, they could get out and about at little cost. The story is told of two West Riding cyclists who decided to relieve the boredom of "doing nowt" by having a run through the Dales. When they reached the top of the first hill, one said to the other: "What's that funny smell?" His friend replied: "I think it's fresh air!"

The cycling clubs had their own Dales stopping places, where refreshments could be bought for a few coppers. One cyclist told me of the effects of a hard day in the Dales on a system that was not too well nourished. The cyclist suffered from "hunger knock", which — if not cured by some food — became a debilitating condition known as "bonk". Mrs. Brown, who had the Post Office at Malham, made some rich fruit cake, and many a cyclist passing through Malhamdale on his or her homeward way stopped to buy a piece. It became known as "Mrs Brown's Anti-Bonk Cake."

A vivid account of the Dales as seen from the saddle of a bike was given to me by Donald Lee, of Keighley. He is still cycling, aged 80 years. He reckons he has covered 300,000 miles on two wheels. Donald became a member of the Keighley Road Club at its first meeting, held in January, 1928, and in 1932 he cycled 695 miles on its Sunday runs, averaging 90 miles a trip. The "CTC Handbook" was the touring cyclist's bible. "In the early 1930s, a cyclist who wanted bed and breakfast was in competition with the driver of an Austin Seven. He belonged to the AA, but carried our Handbook. If you saw him, you'd to beat him to it."

The cyclists of the 1920s toured on "ten bob a day". Those travelling up the Dales pedalled briskly to a point north of Skipton, where they encountered the limestone roads. "These were either dusty or puddly. If you went over Fleet Moss or on any of those high roads, you had lots of gates to open. I seem to remember eight or nine gates across the track from Stainforth to Halton Gill. They were rough roads. It was just as well to learn how to mend a puncture before you set off!"

A summer run would begin at 6 a.m. The starting point at Keighley was "under the clock" (at the old Mechanics' Institute). "When the clock struck six, those of us who were there — went! If anybody was late, they'd to catch us up!" Those on short runs set off much later than the "toughies", who stormed many a hill on the way to the Lakes, to Rievaulx Abbey or to Richmond. One of the cyclists' "tea shops" was Mrs. Falshaw's, Prospect Farm, Buckden. Sam Stables and his wife, at Ashfield, Grassington, kept "open house" for cyclists. "You never let them know you were coming, but they were never caught without food if you popped in." Sometimes, particularly at Grassington, there would be two clubs present at one time. Mrs. Stables rose from her bed at 5-30 a.m. on a Sunday to make Cornish pasties and cakes . . .

On stormy days, the cyclists might go no further than the Mallinsons, of the *Fox and Hounds* at Starbotton, in upper Wharfedale, here to "laik" pontoon for matches; they took their own

ONE OF THE MANY WHO HAS CYCLED ON THE THREE PEAKS: A COMPETITOR IN THE ANNUAL CYCLO-CROSS
EXPRESSES THE JOY OF COMPLETION OF THIS 25 MILE COURSE WHICH INCLUDES 5,000 FEET OF CLIMBING.

pack of cards. Donald sometimes wonders how the caterer made a profit. Mr. Wade, of Halton East, where the cyclists sometimes went to play cards all Sunday afternoon, provided a good fire and had all the lights burning. Yet the Wade family took 8d at the most.

Donald mentions an experience at a Dales cottage visited in 1930. "There was a lad wi' us who allus had a bit more money. He says to the lady at the cottage: 'Can you mek me summat to eat, missus?' She offered to boil him an egg. When he asked the price, she said: 'I'll nobbut charge you a penny for that egg: it wasn't a reight good un."

Cyril Cryer was one of a host of Lancashire cyclists at home in any part of the Dales and who had a special pleasure in following the green tracks across the "tops". Cyril's cycling began in the 1920s and he believed that the coming of the YHA in 1930 was the most significant event for ordinary folk in a time of industrial depression. "At a shilling a night we could afford to go week-ending all through the winter." He loved the simple type of hostel. In the 1930s his annual mileage did not fall short of 10,000. He always stressed that this figure was "moderate" in the cycling world. Some favourite runs were the High Greenfield route from Horton-in-Ribblesdale and the Stake Pass, connecting Semerwater with the top of Kidstones. He liked the many remote ways above Swaledale, also Dead Man's Hill, from Coverdale to Angram, and the Salter Fell route in Bowland. Cyril was a member of an intrepid bunch of cyclists known as the Rough Stuff Fellowship.

In the 1930s, the Dales were being discovered by the working class ramblers of the northern towns. The use of the term "working class" is not meant to be disrespectful. The Dales were being visited in earlier times mainly by middle-class folk — by gentlemen — who had the means and leisure to travel far. G.H.B. Ward, founder of the Clarion Ramblers, described it as "the first Sunday workers' rambling club in the north of England."

Ward, who from 1939 regularly sent *The Dalesman* his "Clarion Handbook", with a friendly letter, described rambling as also being "a culture and a craft . . . an intense love for one's own country, the innermost and the most remote parts of it, the sweetest as well as the wildest, a love for the wind and the rain, the snow and the frost, the hill and the vale, the widest open spaces and the choicest pastoral and arboreal retreats. It is a love for valley and moorsides, their history and their lore, which cannot be exhausted, a love which . . . compels a devotion and adoration which is equal to some men's religion."

At the southern end of the Pennines, the 1930s was the period of running battles with gamekeepers and landowners and of the "mass trespass", which led — after much anguish — to agreements over access to what had previously been well-guarded preserves for grouse and sheep. The Dales country had its preserves which the ramblers wished to share. The West Riding Ramblers' Federation and the Youth Hostels' Association were well represented at a public inquiry in 1934 into the closure of a large grouse moor near Ilkley for periods during grouse nesting and grouse shooting. (The Minister issued an order reducing the period of restriction by one month, which did not satisfy the ramblers and simply made them more than ever keen to have an Access Bill).

In the first volume of *The Dalesman* this fascination with the Great Outdoors was reflected in the articles, including one by Frank S. Smythe, hero of Everest and now confessing that he had undertaken the Three Peaks Walk without completing it. It seems that he first set out to tramp the circuit in 1919. "It was one of my first moutaineering expeditions, if finding a way across lonely and desolate moorlands can count as mountaineering."

William Riley, in a series on Yorkshire's Northern Borderlands, gave an account of "Where Yore is Born" in a style that has not kept very well. He told readers that "the river is born in the

dreary wastes that lie between High Seat and Great Shunner Fell. It is the last word in loneliness when you stand in Hell Gill and let your eyes gaze around. It is a grim and yet a grand scene, and you can well believe that wolves and boars and deer found here one of their last refuges before extermination came." A.J. Brown, in *Broad Acres,* gave an enduring account of the Dales in the 1930s and what it was like to walk when there was the possibility in some areas of not meeting another soul for hours on end.

In 1938, one A. Wainwright set out on a Long Walk. He wrote about his experiences, tucked the manuscript away, brought it out in recent times, when he had become famous for his hand-written, hand-drawn guides to the Lake District and had it published, untouched by sub editor's pencil, in 1986, as *A Pennine Journey.* He climbed Penyghent, exulting mightily; he crossed Foxup Moor, finding "a confusion of sheep-tracks to bewilder the traveller." He used a map to inform and direct; he returned to the map when the journey was over, so that he might live his travels all over again.

Three years before, Tom Stephenson, a keen supporter of the Outdoor movement and champion of ramblers' rights, met two American girls. They had trudged along the 2,000 miles of the Appalachian Trail, in the eastern United States, and now inquired if something of the sort existed in England. Stephenson suggested following a route along the Pennines — a way which Ivor Brown, mindful of the Great North road, was to describe as the Great North Roof — and his suggested route was mentioned in an article he wrote for the *Daily Herald* and published on June 22, 1935.

It was the germ of the idea that led in due course to the establishment of the 250-mile long Pennine Way, the second longest footpath in Britain, extending from Edale in Derbyshire to Kirk Yetholm in Scotland. Many are content to walk a section, the most popular being the 55 miles from Gargrave to the Tan Hill Inn. The Pennine Way was designated in 1951, but not until 1965 was it officially opened by Fred Willey. I recall the joyful scene at a gathering on Malham Moor. (A. Wainwright was to produce *Pennine Way Companion,* in his own inimitable style, and this book would become a best-seller).

John Dower, architect of National Parks, lived in Malhamdale during the war and wrote a series of thoughtful, prophetic articles for *The Dalesman.* The "Dower Report" of 1945 defined a National Park as "an extensive area of beautiful and relatively wild country." The name "Park" was to cause some confusion in a land where it has been used in connection with municipal enterprises in towns. The National Parks were not to be public property and, indeed, ownership would not change on designation.

It was in 1954 that the Dales Park was designated. It extends to 680 square miles and being originally divided almost equally between the North and West Ridings of Yorkshire. (In 1974, boundary changes transferred Dentdale into the new county of Cumbria, but this former tract of Yorkshire remains in the National Park).

The largest outcrop of limestone in Britain occurs in the Yorkshire Dales. From my home at Giggleswick, I look across the Ribble Valley at limestone hills where the rock is not always "limestone grey". In spring, when the sunlight is bright and clear, the limestone is bone-white but the sky holds the blue-black of a "lamb storm". The sky tones are much darker than those of the land, a reversal of what we would normally expect. On a clear evening, as the sun sets grandly over the Bowland moors, I watch the scars become pink, then golden.

Left — A MONTAGE OF PHOTOGRAPHS TAKEN AT THE OFFICIAL OPENING OF THE PENNINE WAY AT MALHAM IN APRIL, 1965. On the picture: Rt. Hon. Fred Willey, Dr. Arthur Raistrick, Tom Stephenson (right) and Wilf Procter, first warden of the West Riding section of the Dales National Park (bottom, centre).

Potholing, as a "sporting science", was introduced to the Dales in August, 1895, when a Frenchman, Edward Alfred Martel, made the first descent of the 340 feet deep main shaft of Gaping Gill using hempen ladders. He went down solo. In the following year an Englishman, Edward Calvert, emulated him. Then — largely through the efforts of the Yorkshire Ramblers' Club — the big open limestone shafts on and around Ingleborough were explored.

The potholers in our photograph were operating in the pre-wet suit period, when any old clothes were "potholing clothes". Boiler suits were chosen by those in the picture, who were in the east passage of the Gaping Gill system. The headlamps were acetylene. On the left is a typical length of hempen rope, with wooden steps. Unless thoroughly dried after every expedition, hemp was weakened by fungal growths.

The first climbers tackled the grit-stone; in the post-1939/45 war period, some hardy pioneers, using much "hardware", began to challenge the limestone faces, such as Malham Cove and the fearsome cliff and overhang at Kilnsey Crag. *Right* – Mabel Sharpe, climbing in 1935, when headgear was a hat or a beret, stuffed with straw. The rope, as for potholing, was made of hemp. *Below* – Tents in a field near Kilnsey Crag, in Wharfedale.

Clapham Church and the war memorial — since removed to another site — have been familiar sights to potholers heading for Clapdale and the underground systems of Ingleborough. The local estate, built up by the Farrers, is sustained energetically by Dr. J.A. Farrer.

For many years, a small charge has been made to walk through the woods in Clapdale, passing the lake and gorge where Reginald Farrer — distinguished plant-collector, artist and writer — planted rhododendrons and bamboos. He had noticed that some Ordovician rock was outcropping in what is generally limestone country, hence the success with rhododendrons.

Clapham, with its information centre and large car park, has a host of trippers in summer and a trickle of dedicated walkers and potholers in winter. The most famous local walk, which includes the woodland path, is known as the Reginald Farrer Trail.

Among the many fine topographers and naturalists associated with the old West Riding, Teesdale was the ultimate goal, attained with some difficulty. They became familiar with the Dales and kept Teesdale forever at the backs of their minds as something special — a valley on the grand scale, with Cross Fell at its head and the water creaming over whin sill at Cauldron Snout and High Force.

At High Force, the River Tees takes a 70 ft. leap into a dark, swirling pool. Sir Walter Scott wrote of the river "rushing madly", leaping "with a ceaseless roar" and then flowing on with a bubbling and hissing. Today, when most visitors have the high mobility of motor transport, High Force retains its appeal. Yet it is the walker who knows it best. He or she, following the Pennine Way northwards, on paths between flower-speckled fields and the wild river, sees tumbling water as the whin sill appears to view. The force of the water gives the impression that the very ground is shaking.

Some Dales personalities. Left – Tot Lord, of Settle, who was an amateur archaeologist, specialising in excavating caves. His best work was done in the 1930s, when he founded the Pig Yard Club, the museum of which eventually incorporated many finds from Victoria Cave. When the Cave Rescue Organisation was formed, Tot was one of the first three wardens. Below, left – A trio at one of many presentations in the best-kept village competition organised by the Yorkshire Rural Community Council. This was for the Lower Dales, and standing by the oak seat from "The Dalesman" is Mrs. Stoddart Scott, of Arthington. Below right – Dr. Arthur Raistrick, outstanding Dales historian and antiquary, with Constance Pearson, the Malhamdale artist.

I have not heard a potholer rhapsodising about the hues of the limestone country, but I have heard joyful sounds as he (sometimes she) went to earth via one of the cracks and crannies that lead to a subterranean world of glistening calcite formations and the everlasting dripping of water from roof into crystal pool. A "pot" is said to come from the Norse. It means a vertical shaft, as opposed to the cave system, which is at or close to the horizontal. Up in Swaledale stands a group of buildings called Crackpot, which is said to mean "the hole where the crows gather". A visitor cannot wait to photograph a friend beside the "Crackpot" fingerpost!

In the west, where the Great Scar Limestone is hundreds of feet thick, the "sporting science" of speleology, known in the Yorkshire Dales as potholing, is a popular sport. There may be 1,000 distinct underground systems, so the devotees have plenty of opportunity to get dirty and wet. It was always a delight to meet W.K. Mattinson at Austwick because he had seen the famous Martel make the first known descent of Gaping Gill's main shaft, on the flanks of Ingleborough. He told of the little Frenchman's preparations, of the way he went down the rope ladder to the edge of the 240 feet shaft and of the anxious wait as he clambered down a hanging ladder until it was established he had reached the floor of a chamber that is of the size of a cathedral. This was the start of a potholing craze. In the following year, an Englishman, Edward Calvert, had reached the floor of the chamber — and returned — using those heavy ladders of wood and hemp.

The Yorkshire Ramblers had an active potholing group and regularly published features about subterranean explorations in their splendid *Journal*. The president, E.E. Roberts, is now regarded as "the last of the gentleman potholers." Reginald Farrer, of Clapham, plant collector, writer and painter, descended Gaping Gill by rope ladder under the auspices of the Ramblers. Another time, a West Craven industrialist called Blackburn Holden descended on a ladder which, naturally, considering the nature of his business, was made of cotton. When it was time to return to the surface, the elasticity of the cotton rope was such that he had trodden on over 20 rungs before he actually left the ground.

By the 1920s — the triumphal 20s — interest had deepened and spread. A Cambridge undergraduate called C.F.D. Long, in one of the most heroic solo journeys underground, explored what became known as White Scar Cave, in Chapel-le-Dale. As a show cave, White Scar has been the means of introducing thousands of layfolk to the glistening underworld of the Yorkshire fells. (For many years, to appease the superstitious nature of Mabel Sharpe, who organised the show cave, I turned up at White Scar on New Year's Day and "let in the New Year", visiting first the pay box and then walking through the system).

Towards the end of the decade, the Craven Pothole Club was formed at Skipton, largely through the energy of Albert Mitchell, the Club emanating from a cycling club known as the Skipton Star Wheelers. Bradford launched a Club in 1933 at a meeting held in Bill Gott's greenhouse. The Northern Cavern and Fell Club, formed as early as 1931, was never large in membership but had a fine spirit and specialised in forcing narrow places. A British Speleological Association was formed at a meeting held in Derbyshire in 1935. One of its prime movers, E. Simpson, then living at Austwick, became its recorder. This organisation was well supported by scientists of national repute.

The Northern Pennine Club, an off-shoot of the BSA, was the first of the post-war Clubs. Just two years after a major discovery, Lancaster Hole on Casterton Fell, the members turned their eyes to Penyghent — and to a stream sink to the south of Glass Moss. They painstakingly explored Penyghent Pot to a depth of over 500 feet. Cave diving had begun in the Dales as early as 1940, when the BSA met in Kingsdale. Members entered a small hole lying to the west of

"The Dalesman" has richly augmented the library of the region by publishing books of local interest, of which these are good examples. "The Old Hand-Knitters of the Dales" was suggested to Marie Hartley and Joan Ingilby by Harry J. Scott, founder of the magazine. Norman Thornber's "Pennine Underground", was the first guide of its kind, presenting each notable underground system in fine detail. Edmund Cooper, whose special interest was Swaledale, wrote extensively about family life in the upper valley.

Rowten Pot — and "pushed" it to a depth of 395 feet below the entrance, including passages with a combined length of a quarter of a mile.

It pleased me to compile and publish an account of man's involvement with the Yorkshire caves and potholes (*The Hollow Mountains,* 1961). In this work I had the support of Norman Thornber, who had for years anonymously written "Dales Farmer's Diary" in the magazine. Norman's great contribution to potholing was his handbook listing in fine detail all the known caves and the tackle needed to explore them. He was one of the original wardens of the Cave Rescue Organisation, established in February, 1935, after a winter of talk and planning. The other wardens were Reg. Hainsworth of Ingleton; Godfrey Wilson of Stainforth; and Tot Lord of Settle.

The CRO has had considerable success in recovering potholers (and occasionally sheep and lambs) from deep and narrow places. My own favourite story of rescue in the Dales is that of May, 1910, when Mr. W.F. Boyd, a member of the Yorkshire Ramblers' Club, fell and broke his thigh in Sunset Hole, Chapel-le-Dale. He was carried out of the system on a table leaf which had to be trimmed so often in the negotiation of narrow passages and awkward bends that it took on the shape of the casualty, who was helpless underground for 17 hours.

In this brief review of the discovery of the Dales, the naturalists and antiquaries should not be forgotten. They include some outstanding working-class naturalists of the industrial towns whose leisure time was limited but who became authorities in their chosen fields. The Kearton brothers, born and reared in Swaledale but soon domiciled in the South, were already famous as early popularisers of natural history. They had used the new half-tone process of block-making to illustrate their natural history books with real photographs; they visited outlandish places and wrote up their experiences interestingly. Richard and Cherry did not forget their native dale and enjoyed returning to it.

A charming book published in 1930, *Silva Gars* (Grass Wood), by John Crowther, the Grassington antiquary, was concerned with the Wood's "history, antiquities, ancient footpaths, wild flowers and wildlife, together with a guide to twenty-seven interesting walks in the district, with maps and illustrations." It was dedicated to those 18 Grassington youths who had been killed during the 1914–18 war. When *Silver Gars* appeared, readers were not surprised to find biological facts and local hymns, a list of birds and an account of the Stubbs family, for the age of specialisation, of widespread professionalism was some years in the future. (I once heard a Dales farmer say of a pretentious scientist: "yon fellow was eddicated till he's ignorant"). Crowther, who had a little chemist's shop at Grassington, with an adjacent wooden hut forming a museum, reported anything of interest to the Press and appears to have enjoyed his status as a celebrity.

Such works as Halliwell Sutcliffe's highly romantic *The Striding Dales* still has enormous appeal among the middle-aged and elderly. The Foreword gives a foretaste of things to come and should be set to organ music: "The Yorkshire highlands, raking up to wide-flung mountain fastnesses, lie remote from usual haunts; and their people are rooted in free, unspoiled acres. There is only the one road to knowledge of the Dales and Dalesfolk — lifelong intimacy with the rugged scarps, the hidden glens, the homesteads, big and little, perched on the mountains' feet or gathered into grey, comely villages . . ."

The Sutcliffe book was illustrated by the subtle watercolours of A. Reginald Smith. *Malham and Malham Moor*, by Arthur Raistrick, published by *Dalesman* in 1947 was illustrated no less sensitively by Constance Pearson. She portrayed the area in all weathers, not least under grey skies, and she did not shy away from the portrayal of figures — the lean figures of Dales farmers, engaged in their seasonal occupations like sheep-clipping and haytiming. Dr. Raistrick, in his

CHRIS CHEETHAM, OUTSTANDING NATURALIST, WHO SPENT MOST OF HIS LONG LIFE AT AUSTWICK, PICTURED IN 1954. HE WAS SECRETARY OF THE YORKSHIRE NATURALISTS' UNION.

many articles and books, has set a high standard by which any work on the Dales will be judged. The Malham work sprang from the discoveries of a local study group and is dedicated to local men, Abraham Banks and Gilbert Brown.

Field Meets of the Yorkshire Naturalists' Union introduced the members to the limestone pavements, indigenous woods, tarns like Malham and Semerwater and the remnants of old mossland, as in the Lawkland area. The records made in the field were meticulously recorded and published. In this respect, ornithologists were to be grateful to Ralph Chislett. When the Union attained its centenary in 1961, he wrote: "In considering ornithologically the hundred years of the Union's existence, several matters call for comment, notably the changes from the times of private collecting of specimens to those of recording occurrences with detailed notes written at the time, and of securing quick confirmation of facts if possible and expert concurrence later." (Naturalists recall Chislett each March when a Memorial Lecture is delivered in Leeds).

The Craven Naturalists and Scientific Association, which is over a century old, and the younger Wharfedale Naturalists, are among the many organisations that have led an active existence in the Dales as well as arranging winter lectures. The small and now defunct Austwick Field Club, of which I was a member, could draw on the experience and skill of naturalists like Chris. Cheetham and W.K. Mattinson. The former had a species of daddy longlegs named after him!

Records show considerable changes in the Dales — the coming of the big upland conifer forests, extensive ploughing and re-seeding of meadowland with ryegrass and the gripping [mechanical draining] of the moors, leading to unsightly erosion and rivers coming rapidly into spate. There have been gains, not least the return of the roe deer to the Dales woods, of the sika deer — strays from Bowland — to some far western parts of the Dales and the re-establishment of red deer by a farmer at Long Preston. The first red stag ventured into Upper Wharfedale as the Ice Age ameliorated thousands of years ago. The last local stag was slain in the early 1930s. With several companions it had been too venturesome and strayed from the old deer park on the hill into the deciduous woods by the Wharfe. The move made sense to the stag but infuriated the foresters, for red stags have a habit of bole-scoring trees or browsing the foliage. At one time 13 mounted heads might be found at Bolton Hall, but the collection was dispersed. There is one at the Rectory, which is now the home of the estate agent. Another adorns a wall at Barden Tower which, appropriately, was the old hunting lodge of the Cliffords of Skipton Castle, being their base in the Forest of Barden. Wild red deer, inseparably linked with the feudal period, were too large and conspicuous to survive in the free-ranging state when the feudal age had passed. The last deer are recalled by Dr. Arthur Raistrick. In the 1930s, one of his good friends was Arthur Waters, whose father looked after the deer. "We saw them fairly often."

Enter the *Rose and Crown* at Bainbridge, and you see varnished fish, in varnished cases, with expressionless stares and brief details about where and when they were caught. Dick Chapman used to tell me about fishing in the river Bain, the shortest river in England. He spoke sadly of the decline of the mayfly hatch, which once was an exciting spectacle, causing the brown trout to feed voraciously. There would be several species of newly-hatched flies and the most successful angler was he who changed the artificial flies on his cast to suit the latest hatches. About half way up the Bain was the place to see a real hatch of mayflies. From May to autumn, the big hatches of flies clouded the air above the Bain. But no longer . . .

Left – Tom Varley, drystone waller, photographed when he was living at Stainforth in North Ribblesdale and was making a name for himself as a craftsman. Happily, the highway authority, when improving a stretch of road or making a by-pass, arranges for traditional mortarless walls to be constructed.

The Pennine walls, which are among the Seven Wonders of the North, make an immediate appeal to first-time visitors to the Dales, who marvel at the extent and durability of the wall pattern. Craftsmanship with stone of the same high order is to be seen in old structures, such as the areas where lead was mined and where the remains include the well-masoned arches of mine adits and a range of utilitarian buildings.

Right – M'duke Miller, "mine host" of "The Falcon" at Arncliffe, in Littondale, also a notable artist, with a preference for water-colours. He had a great feeling for his native dale, which he liked to call Amerdale. He would mention that where the Skirfare, river of the dale, meets the Wharfe, the name is Amerdale Dub, and he was fond of quoting Wordsworth's poem about the White Doe of Rylstone, in which there is mention of the "deep fork of Amerdale".

Dales faces. Above, left – Arnold Brown, guide to Ingleborough Cave, near Clapham. He was fond of playing tunes on the stalactites, using the key to the entrance door. He provided each visitor with candles on quaint three-pronged holders. Above – Dalesman at a sheep show. Left – Chris Chapman, of Hawes, who spent his working life in the grocery trade and was fond of recalling his early years when he went out delivering groceries with horse and cart.

Christopher Timothy has played the part of James Herriot since 1974, when the BBC first recorded a series based on the best-selling novels of a vet's life in the Yorkshire Dales — television programmes which have been seen throughout the world. For many people, Yorkshire has become Herriotshire.

The photograph (above) is of the actor Christopher Timothy, standing against an old car at Marsett, near Semerwater. On that day, the filming had been delayed because a local sow would not farrow on cue!

The veterinary surgeon who used the pen-name James Herriot for his recollections of Dales life in the 1930s was born in Weardale but reared in Glasgow. When he first came to Yorkshire, he expected to find a seedy, industrialised county. He was amazed at the grandeur of the Dales scenery.

During a journey across the moors from Leyburn to Grinton, he stopped the car and stood, spellbound, at the sight of rolling heather moors encompassing narrow green valleys that the Norsemen of old called "dales". He frequently visits the Pennine dales, while living almost in the shadow of the Hambleton Hills. From the top of Sutton Bank, in clear weather, he can look westwards and see — Pen Hill, one of the highspots in Wensleydale.

HERRIOT COUNTRY

A YOUNG VET named Alf White experienced life in the Dales in the 1930s. Years later, he jotted down recollections of that period in a series of light-hearted books, using the pen-name James Herriot. These books, and the films based upon them, have achieved considerable success in every part of the world.

Herriot is now as closely associated with the old North Riding dales as is Wordsworth with Lakeland and the Brontës with the peaty moors above Haworth. We have all become familiar with Skeldale House, on which the veterinary practice was based. We know about James himself, also his wife Helen, the irascible Siegfried Farnon and his wayward younger brother, Tristan; plus a severe-looking but basically kindly housekeeper.

Herriot offers us some striking characterisations of Dalesfolk, plus lots of ailing beasts and an unruly mob of dogs that bounces off the front door in their excitement whenever anyone calls. When I asked a Dales farmer about conditions in the 1930s, he simply replied: "Read yon fellow Herriot." His neighbour wrily observed: "In the 1930s, I couldn't afford a vet!" When I parked my car against the churchyard wall at Askrigg, an American was taking a photograph of Cringley House, just across the road, the exterior of which was used by the BBC. "Gee," said the American in wonderment.

What was intended by Herriot as a simple record of Dales experiences is a boon to local tourism. The Herriot Country — mainly Swaledale and Wensleydale, taking in the little tributary valleys — attracts crowds of visitors who are trying to capture the special flavour of these enchanting books by being in the settings that inspired them. Herriot's name is everywhere, from a cafe to the title on a guide book. Down at Richmond they have a museum in which is preserved the BBC "set" for the vet's consulting room.

Whenever I lecture about the Dales, and seek instant rapport with a roomful of strangers, I usually allow Herriot to introduce me by telling a story about him. My early slides show places used in the introduction of the BBC series *All Creatures Great and Small* — the bridge at Langthwaite, near Reeth, and the water-splash on the moorland road between Arkengarthdale and Swaledale.

My one brief encounter with James Herriot confirmed an impression I had that he remains a quiet, self-effacing man. The occasion of the meeting was a gathering in Leeds to mark the publication of what became the best-selling *James Herriot's Yorkshire*. Also at the gathering was his wife, the Helen of the book. He married her at Thirsk parish church, and they drove into Wensleydale for a honeymoon spent at *The Wheatsheaf*, Carperby, a honeymoon mainly devoted to the tuberculin testing of cattle! I met the author's real-life son, Jimmy, who is also a vet. I was introduced to the originals of Siegfried and Tristan [the Sinclair brothers] plus their spouses. Three men and three wives were still the very best of friends. The warmth of that friendship spread to whoever was introduced to them.

It was Mrs. Herriot — er, Joan White — who encouraged her husband to jot down his memories. He was "turned fifty" before he began to write about the "wonderland" he discovered as a young city-bred vet when he moved to Thirsk and had sorties into the nearest Pennine dales. He had the usual early frustrations of the author. The story he eventually related was somewhat fictionalised but charmed us all. The first book opened with the young vet's arrival at Darrowby, which is a composite town, "a bit of Thirsk, something of Richmond, Leyburn and Middleham, and a fair chunk of my imagination." He has explained that one evening, as he typed, he also glanced at a football match on television. James Herriot was the goalkeeper for Birmingham. The name sounded pleasant, there were no Herriots in the Veterinary Register — "so that was it."

James Herriot bemoans in his Yorkshire book the passing of the old type of Yorkshire farmer — the man who possessed half a dozen cows, treated them with black magic remedies and spoke the Yorkshire dialect. One suspects that he most enjoys his solitary, never lonely, walks across the Pennine uplands. "The high country is too bleak for some people, but it is up there on the empty moors, with the curlews crying, that I have been able to find peace and tranquillity of mind."

Mr. Herriot's books deserve their success, though people — having read them — are inclined to think of the Dales themselves as they used to be. Herriot has himself referred to his luck in deciding to write several books rather than trying to pack the experiences of the 1930s into a single volume. Three cinema films and a number of television series ensured that his work would be generally known.

Whatever we might think of the notion, the Dales have become "Herriot Country" to most of the visitors and the films commend its beauty as well as the characteristics of the Dalesfolk to people the world over. Herriot, it seems, had felt that the first films did not show enough of the Dales. He is happy with the BBC's approach to the work. And in the end, the mind retains vivid pictures of dale, moor and fell; of greystone village and farmsteads tied to each other by the walls that form a futuristic pattern on the landscape. It is a social record, too, of a time when both farmer and vet did their best to alleviate animal suffering without knowing much about the cause or the most efficacious treatment.

The Dales farmers have prospered, though they are unlikely to admit it. A land agent said: "They used to come down in the war and say: 'I've got a form; what shall I do with it?'" We dealt with them, but by degrees they got to know every subsidy that was going and how to claim it. They have got their cars; there was hardly a car in the district up to the war — very few anyway. They bicycled or walked or went by train . . . I love to see the farmers flourishing. Where there were two horses there is now probably three tractors and a Land Rover — and a private car." They are very highly mechanised. At Keld, in Swaledale, a friend thought hard and long when I asked him who had the first tractor in the upper dale. Then he thought it might have been Percy Metcalfe, of Crackpot Hall, a "little grey Fergie" (Ferguson), which he bought from Prestons of Bainbridge. And that was after the war.

The hill farming grant was of considerable importance in the Dales. It was this grant that provided the head of money to put up new buildings, to cover the cost of installing electricity, to improve water supplies and also to modernise the farmhouses. The old "black ranges" were succeeded by the AGA or Raeburn stoves. The old farmhouse was, on the whole, warm and dry, with a fire maintained throughout the year for cooking, heating water as well as infusing some heat into large, cold rooms.

Tradition is still an important feature of Dales life, as I realised once again when attending the 87th annual show of the Swaledale Open Agricultural and Horticultural Society. This was a

ALERT COLLIES IN THE DALES — AT LANGTHWAITE (ABOVE) AND HORTON-IN-RIBBLESDALE (BELOW).

DALES STRUCTURES: ABOVE – ANCIENT THATCHED HOUSE, FORMERLY AT HURST. BELOW – IVELET BRIDGE, WHICH CROSSES THE SWALE IN A SINGLE, HIGH ARCH.

thoroughly local event and not some idea dreamed up by a publicity officer. The steward at the gate collected my £1, stamped my hand with the word "Muker" and smiled as a nearby farmer said to me: "Thoo wants to be thankful he didn't clip a bit out of an ear." Judging the sheep proceeded along traditional lines. If the judges were over-awed by the presence of some of the keenest flockmasters in the North they did not show it. A young judge had already developed the art of dallying so that everyone was kept in suspense.

The judges took in the general characteristics of the sheep and then moved closer, parting the wool, testing its quality and looking for "black bits". Ewes suffered a total loss of dignity when they were turned on their backs, then reared into a sitting position, where their bellies sagged. The teats of the animals in this class were carefully examined, for they must not have suckled young. "A judge wants to see if t'tits is reight," said a friendly farmer at my right elbow. "Some tits can be duds".

The show catalogue included a note: "Luncheons for all officials at 12-30 p.m." In the village hall, trestle tables had been joined together and covered with food. It formed the sort of Yorkshire meal that J.B. Priestley had in mind when he described West Riding life before the First World War. At Muker, each diner settled down to beef and ham, lettuce and pickles, followed by trifle and cream, meringue, apple pie and cream cakes. Coffee was available and there was a choice of port or sherry. It was good to tour the tents and see produce of all kinds, also to watch some competitions, including a modern variant — welly-throwing. One of the competitors spent five minutes ramming the sides into the foot of the wellington, which he threw with such force the missile almost went into orbit. "Screwed-up wellies" were pronounced illegal!

At the sheep pens, the farmers continued to discuss the fine points about sheep. A latecomer arrived. "Hoo is ta?" said one man, to be told: "All is safely gathered in. Taties oot and cows laid in." The supreme champion of the show came from a prize-winning flock at Sleightholme, near Bowes. The owner had paid £16,000 for it at the autumn sales.

Meanwhile, the attention of the crowd had switched to the fell-tops, where runners in the senior fell race were displaying their prowess. A Land Rover had been driven to the skyline so that a check might be kept on the competitors. The vehicle was parked at an elevation of about 1,500ft with a patch of light visible between the chassis and the ground.

So had an old Dales event remained true to the spirit of its founders while absorbing a few modern notions?

The percentage of true Dalesfolk in the community declines as young people — unable to find suitable employment or to afford to buy a home in their native areas — move off to the towns. Remaining in the villages is a population that shows its age. In the 1930s, a couple hoped to begin their life together on some little old place on the fellside. As they scrimped and saved, they were able to move to better places. Alas, they can no longer afford modern rents or expenditure on capital items like machinery. In any case, large numbers of holdings have been amalgamated and others devoted to growing conifers. Milk production has virtually ceased at the daleheads, where in some cases the cattle are ranched. So we have the spectacle of ruined farmsteads and walls gapped in so many places it looks as though the fell has been castellated.

Lower down the dale, the milk producers have experienced the trauma of milk quotas, to ease the EEC's embarrassment over its massive agricultural budget. A Dales farmer who said he had no money left later ruefully confessed that he had bought additional land for £40,000 — and, on the introduction of quotas had to spend thousands more to buy a greater allocation to enable him to turn milk cattle on to that land. Encouraged to find alternative means of making an income,

*The Written Word. Top – J. Fairfax-
Blakeborough lived in Westerdale, on the
North York Moors, but wrote a good deal
about the Dales. He described himself as a
"ruralist". Above – Thomas Armstrong,
author of long novels, including "Adam
Brunskill", for which he researched Dales
lead-mining to the extent of becoming an
authority on the industry! Right – Sir
Rupert Hart-Davis, notable author and
publisher, who for years had a holiday
cottage high on Kisdon, Swaledale, and
now lives at Marske, near Richmond.*

some farmers have converted barns into "bunk barns", with kitchens, for letting to visitors. Many a farm sports a "bed and breakfast" sign. I know a farmer's daughter who is an expert on computers and has written a large number of books for sale to enthusiasts. Her own collection of computers is housed in an upper room — "where, years ago, a Dales family would try to make some extra money — spinning or weaving cloth with a handloom!"

One of the best-known estates on the Pennine dales is the far-flung Raby estate, which extends to the head of Teesdale, on the north bank. Until the boundary review of 1974, land south of the river was in Yorkshire. Part of the appeal of the Raby farmhouses is that they are regularly white-washed, the white showing up conspicuously against the lush greens of the dale and the russet tones of the fells.

The agent for Lord Barnard and I discussed an upper Dales characteristic — the dual economy of mining and farming. They were closely integrated in the economies of many local families. When lead mining declined in Teesdale during the first 20 years of this century, Lord Barnard kept the farms pretty much as they were, resisting the temptation to amalgamate them and create large, more viable holdings. If amalgamation took place, he said, an unacceptably large number of redundant farm buildings and some decline in the population of the dale would be experienced.

There are 80 farmhouses in the upper dale and a heavy maintenance programme is needed. Every effort is made to use local materials, such as the Teesdale greystone roofing slate. Many upper Teesdale farms are made of limestone, with some whinstone; the walls may be up to two feet thick and unfortunately many of them are damp, the stone being porous. No deadening uniformity exists in the type of building to be seen in the upper dale. Part of the enchantment of the area is in the architectural variety, yet unity is preserved by the white-washed walls.

Among my photographs of the Dales is a picture of a bouquet of flowers being held by a farmer's wife. Those blooms were not pampered greenhouse varieties, neither had they been grown in neat rows to satisfy urban markets. The woman had been on her way from the fields to the kitchen to prepare some food for the next meal, when she passed a meadow that had just been mown. Among the felled grasses were flowers — maybe 20 species of flowers. She impulsively gathered a few and now they rested together in a delightful tonal harmony.

With modern ploughing, re-seeding, intensive fertilisation and close-cutting of grass for silage, a Dales meadow is now as visually interesting as a billiards table, yet there is some hope for the remaining old-fashioned hay meadows, such as that from which the farmer's wife gathered blooms for her bouquet. A welfare scheme for "environmentally sensitive areas" in the Pennine Dales has had an encouraging response from farmers who have been paid to pursue agricultural methods that maintain the traditional beauty and wildlife of the area. It is a voluntary scheme, under which the farmer is paid £40 an acre. In return he agrees to maintain the drystone walls and the barns. He limits fertilisation and forgoes pesticides. It is also understood that he will not cut the meadows until a set date. By this time the meadow flowers should have seeded, ensuring the continuation of their kind.

The Dales National Park gives generous grants towards tree planting and woodland management schemes. Examples are the replacement of diseased elms at Parcevall Hall, Skyreholme, and a replanting scheme at the Lower Falls, Aysgarth, to help to recreate continuous woodland on both banks of the Ure. In this patching up of ravages in the Dales landscapes, the Park Committee has a Three Peaks Project, concerned with the famous footpath that takes in the summits of Whernside, Ingleborough and Penyghent. In places, oozing peat bog has been so disturbed by the boots of thousands of walkers, plus the runners and cyclists in the annual springtime foot race and autumnal cyclo-cross, the area looks like a tract of Flanders in the 1914–18 war.

When I first walked the Three Peaks, there were areas where I could not be sure where the path ran, so slight was the effect of the few walkers on the area. On the last occasion, I set off from Horton, clomped up wooden steps on the steep "nose end" of Penyghent and, during the descent along the Pennine Way, was appalled by the extent of the damage. Near Churn Milk Hole on Penyghent, the trampled width was 20 metres, with a completely bare width of four metres down the centre. Using a Swedish-manufactured chemical called "Solidry", the project team has created a two-metre wide path through the boggy area. Vegetation has begun to return to the damaged areas on either side.

The upsurge in the number of visitors to the Dales has been dramatic. Yellow traffic lines have appeared at Bolton and Barden. Car parks have been made near the Strid, on the river bank near the Cavendish Pavilion and also in the village (where there is also a new hall, a splendid venue for old-time dancing!). In one year, 30,000 people followed the Strid nature trail.

It is estimated that a million people visit Malham each year. Recalling my own first visits, to take services at the little chapel, is not easy today, when the Chapel is cheek-by-jowl with a large information centre, which stands near a permanently sterilised area that serves as a car park. Now a flight of steps has been made beside Malham Cove and, let it be whispered, there was talk of fitting wooden steps in the waterfall area of Gordale Scar.

At the head of Teesdale, between 55,000 and 70,000 people a year use the Water Authority's tarmac path from a car park (complete with toilet block) to the head of Caldron Snout. With up to 120 people on the path at a time if the weather is good, it is no wonder that the local grouse are particularly confiding. Around Caldron Snout, the vegetation is trampled, the rocks boot-scored and duck-boards have been fitted to the "soft spots" lower down. Aysgarth is a "honeypot". The roadside bank of the Wharfe near Yockenthwaite looks like Blackpool Promenade on a hot day in summer and, in similar conditions, there may be a carnival atmosphere at Ribblehead.

What I could never have foreseen when I first knew the Dales was the green prairie, with wall-to-wall ryegrass; the making of Big Bale Silage in the Wet, with spray rising from the tractor wheels; the marketing of Swaledale cheese at Hawes; the sad run-down of the Settle–Carlisle railway; and the neglect of walls and outbarns as farmers concentrated their stock in huge buildings close to the farmhouse. The National Park Officer, who is anxious to work with local people in the maintenance of this heritage, has said: "Unless we can find an acceptable solution and make significant progress within the next five to 10 years, this distinctive landscape may have gone beyond the point of no return."

For the moment, we can rejoice that so much in the Dales continues to give us pleasure. I remember seeing daffodils in a garden at Hawes — and looking up to where patches of snow adorned the high fells. I recall the flute-like clarity of the ring ouzel's song in the echo-chamber of the gill below the Buttertubs and a Maytime ride down Swaledale, amid 1,000 shades of green, with the sun bringing a sparkle to the river. My list of special pleasures also includes the white water pouring over the Yoredale rocks at Aysgarth, a distant view of Hubberholme Church from Horsehead Pass and, of course, the curlew's song-flight, with the bird's wings stiff and arched like a kite, the bubbling sounds flooding the whole parish . . .

The Dales have been in a process of change since they were gouged out of an ancient plateau by rushing water and the relentless movement of glacial ice. For many centuries, the conditions have permitted people to settle here, to raise families, to tend cattle — to live, to love, to die. In due course, the ice will return, and the process will start all over again . . .

A WALKER DESCENDS FROM PENYGHENT TOWARDS HULL POT AND HORTON-IN-RIBBLESDALE.

DON THOMSON WITH AN AXE HEAD HE MADE AVAILABLE AS THE TROPHY IN THE FIRST "FELLSMAN" HIKE WHICH ANNUALLY ATTRACTS HUNDREDS OF TOUGH WALKERS TO THE WESTERN FELLS. THE PHOTOGRAPH WAS TAKEN IN GRASSINGTON MARKET PLACE.

SEMERWATER, ABOUT WHICH THERE IS AN ANCIENT TALE OF A DROWNED SETTLEMENT.

WROUGHT IRON HEADPIECE ON THE GRAVE OF WILF HOGGART IN THE
CHURCHYARD AT EAST MARTON. THE PIECE WAS MADE BY HIS
ASSISTANT, JIMMY THOMPSON.